La Casa Adobe

WILLIAM·LUMPKINS

Revised and Enlarged Edition

Ancient City Press
Santa Fe, New Mexico
1986

International Standard Book Number:
0-941270-34-3
Library of Congress Catalogue Number:
86-071415

Printed in the United States of America

Third Printing
Second Edition

CONTENTS

PREFACE TO THE FIRST EDITION, 1961

This book would never have been published if the Russians had remained a backward, aristocracy-ridden, agrarian nation. This may sound strange, and it is. But in the early 1960s I saw a movie on modern Russia, and within the week read an article by an American newsman who had visited Russia after twelve years. The movie showed the man-in-the-street in Russia, and her great military and air power. This appalled me—not the air or military— but the people, because here were millions of men and women trying to dress and act like the average American. Not only their dress but all their dreary, conforming automobiles, streets, buildings were Main-Street-America. Then the article by the newsman, telling of his great joy and surprise at finding the Russians, after twelve years, had discarded their native dress. And he remarked, "I couldn't tell them from the American tourist; even the shoes were good." He was pleased. I was appalled.

Then I decided to do my small part in trying to turn this tidal wave of grey, dull, uninspired sameness. This, all of a sudden, becomes a far greater danger than wars, bombs, atomic fallout and germ warfare. The same thing, I realized with clarity, was happening to architecture, my profession. The International School stretches from the Atlantic to the Pacific in a great stack of uninspired architecture, with California ranch houses between. In the Southwest, with adobe as a material, there is the possibility of extending the nucleus of a revolt—a regional resistance to conformity. The material is a good material, plastic and easily worked, with great potential for original space enclosures. The young architect working in this area should re-examine his or her little box of tricks, learned from what is now the academy of conformity: the American Architectural School. Architects should open their eyes and look at the countryside and at the native architecture and begin to create a truly original form, based on adobe and the climate of the Southwest. They should throw away their handbooks of California Contemporary Architecture and their books from the Bauhaus Group and look and see themselves in relation to the country in which they are living, and create for these people an architecture which is original and adapted to the country.

The client, the family establishing a homestead in the Southwest, should demand of their architect a house to fit the great plains and mountains, the vast blue skies and huge cottonwood trees. The experience of living in an adobe house is like no other. There is a great security, a peace, a belonging that comes over the family which dwells long in these thick walled enclosures. And let the newcomer to the Southwest not be fooled by the fake adobe, built of stud frames with a silly curve at the top of the firewall, or the hard concrete block which at best forms a ridiculous imitation of adobe.

Adobe is a sculptural material. The wise architect will use it to create buildings unlike any others—truly individual, original and belonging to the country and the people who inhabit it.

La Casa Adobe presents some sketches and drawings of adobe houses inspired by existing old houses in and around Santa Fe, New Mexico, in the hope that younger and more vigorous architects will use this source of material to develop contemporary forms suitable for living in the years to come. The rush to the "International" style in architecture during its revolutionary period was very good as a catalyst to clean the drawing boards of the "mish-mash" of Classical Architecture and return modern man to a fundamental concept of space enclosure. Now that the International style is the accepted academy, the repetition of its form by ungifted architects is producing in America a sterile architecture worse than the "gingerbread" it replaced. Now is the time for the architect-designer to look at the diversity and wealth of materials inherent in the American building tradition and return space enclosure to a truly creative art. The adobe house of the Southwest is here—a source of material, different and well suited to the climatic demands of the Southwest. Use it.

I hope that with this small book gifted men and women will turn to adobe—not synthetic adobe, hollow tile, concrete block, or brick covered with stucco to form a rigid, poor imitation of adobe, but the real material formed of the native earth and blending and belonging in the vast landscape of the Southwest.

La Jolla, California   William Lumpkins
1961

PREFACE TO THE SECOND EDITION, 1986

Early in the 1970s, with the oil embargo, solar heating began to be explored as an alternative to fossil fuels. The early movement was centered in Santa Fe and New Mexico. Many methods to provide human comfort in enclosed spaces were tried. Much work and resarch went into establishing mass materials that would store heat and return it to enclosed spaces when the sun was not shining. Members of Santa Fe's study group, the Sun Mountain Solar Group, conducted experiments and wrote papers to extend pioneer work at the Massachusetts Institute of Technology and the University of Arizona and in France.

To understand the Passive Solar Heating system one must realize that the human body is a "heat-machine." It has to give off a certain amount of heat each minute of the day and night. This heat flows out from the skin to solid materials. In the air around a person there is very little that will absorb or receive this heat. Usually it must travel until a solid mass is encountered. If the mass is thin, as in plastered walls, the heat rapidly moves through to the colder side. With insulation it is returned back into the space. If there are masses around the person with the ability to absorb the body-emitted heat, then, if the temperature of the mass is low it will absorb heat at a rapid rate so the body feels cold. If the mass is slightly warm (in the 50-degree Fahrenheit range) the body heat loss is balanced and one feels comfortable in a rather wide range of air temperature. Thus the program for Passive Solar Heating is to expose the mass to the warming rays of the sun during the day and, as stated, "charge" the mass for nighttime release.

Passive Solar Heating generally falls into three categories: Direct Gain, Greenhouse, and Trombe. The Direct Gain system creates an overabundance of glass along the south wall with floors and walls of mass material. The Greenhouse or Sun Porch system puts the glass outside of the house area with a mass wall between the living space and the sun trap area.

The third system, first developed by Dr. Trombe in France, places a mass wall along the south side of the building and installs glass in front of the wall. In the original, there were air slots along the floor line and at the ceiling to allow the colder air along the floor to be drawn into the space between the glass and the wall and through the force of thermal air movement up along the wall, absorbing the heat and discharging the air into the space at the ceiling slots. In examining this system it became apparent that if the slots were omitted the mass would gain and store a great amount of heat, which would be radiated into the living space. This proved to be the more effective system.

Many fine books explaining in detail the various systems are available. It is only important to remember that glass plus mass will produce an environment that is compatible to human comfort.

All mass materials will receive and store heat. Water will store the greatest amount of heat per volume unit, with solid concrete, masonry, stone, and adobe following in descending order. In looking at water's ability to store heat, several early systems used walls of metal tanks, metal drums, and finally hollow concrete. These sytems provide the greatest amount of heat storage and delivery to interior spaces.

Why, then, adobe? While its storage capacity is slightly less than concrete or solid masonry, its virtues far outweigh this defect. Adobe absorbs heat at a slower rate, but it also emits heat at a slower rate and provides a longer heating period. And of course it is a natural material which depletes none of the fossil fuels and is available in almost all the sunbelts of the world.

Adobe is simply a balanced mix of clay and sand. If there is too much sand the adobe crumbles when dry; if too much clay, it shrinks and cracks. A few trial runs develop the correct mix. Best of all, if you want a basement, then the material for the adobe is right on the building site.

This second edition of *La Casa Adobe* has been brought up to date by the addition of drawings for four solar adobe houses. The entire text has also undergone minor editorial revision.

Santa Fe, New Mexico   William Lumpkins
1986

ABOUT THE AUTHOR

William Lumpkins, now a practicing architect in Santa Fe, New Mexico, is a native New Mexican. He grew up in the New Mexico which was just entering statehood, on ranches where adobe was the standard, accepted building material. In his early youth he saw many of the surviving fine examples of great Southwest adobe architecture.

In old Lincoln, all the buildings were intact. Nearby Fort Stanton was a living museum of the Territorial style, built by army engineers, many of whom were architects by profession. These great adobe structures, thick-walled and lime-plastered with accurately detailed Colonial trim, were a part of Lumpkins's youth.

In the mid-twenties he visited Galisteo, the Athens of New Mexico as it has often been called. He remembers vividly the old town before the depression of the thirties almost destroyed it through neglect when the inhabitants moved on to find work.

Later, in the early thirties, Lumpkins first studied architecture with Irvin Parsons, one of the first architects to make use of the adobe house as a source of inspiration for his many finely designed homes in and around Santa Fe. Parsons influenced Lumpkins more than any of the others with whom he later studied and through the years the former has remained a mainspring of inspiration in his work.

INTRODUCTION

The first settlers in New Mexico came from Mexico and Spain in the late sixteenth and early seventeenth centuries. Don Juan de Onate colonized the area above presentday Espanola in 1598, some one hundred years after Columbus had first sighted the Americas and almost seventy years after Cortez conquered Mexico.

These early colonists came from a Spain only recently feeling the results of the wealth of the New World flowing into and enriching the country. Previous to this, Spain was a frontier of the Old World: rural and backward. The common building material was adobe (sun-dried brick), as it had been for centuries in the Mediterranean world. The early settlers of New Mexico were completely familiar with adobe construction methods, which had been developed over a period of six to eight thousand years by the Moors, who came to Spain in the fifth century and brought the system with them from Egypt and the Middle East.

Vitruvius, a Roman architect writing about the time of Nero, describes brick. I feel certain that he is describing sun-dried brick because later he speaks of burned bricks.

> Beginning with brick, I shall state of what kind of clay they ought to be made. They should not be made of sandy or pebbly clay or of fine gravel, because when made of these kinds they are in the first place heavy, and secondly, when washed by the rains as they stand in walls, they go to pieces and break up and the straw [even at this time straw was used to make adobe] in them does not hold together, on account of the roughness of the material.

We easily recognize this early "recipe" for adobe as it was described almost two thousand years ago by Vitruvius. His book was a standard handbook for architects of the Mediterranean world well into the time of the early Spanish settlers of New Mexico.

In his handbook Vitruvius also discusses the protection of the top of the adobe wall with burned brick:

> It has now been explained how limitations of building space necessarily forbid the employment of brick [sun-dried walls within the city. When it becomes necessary to use them outside the city they should be constructed as follows, in order to be perfect and durable. On the top of the wall, lay a structure of *burnt* brick, about a foot and a half in height, under the tile and projecting like a coping.

This description rather accurately describes the ornamental brick coping used in the Territorial style of architecture in New Mexico.

The journals of Coronado and others who left a written record of the first exploration of New Mexico speak of the Pueblo Indian buildings with no great surprise or curiosity as to their being constructed of sun-dried mud. Their only reference is to a difference in method of construction.

The earliest descriptions are by Pedro de Castaneda and Mota Padilla,[1] who were with Coronado during the first exploration in 1540-42. Cibola, one of the Zuni villages, was first described by Castaneda:

> It is a little, crowded village, looking as if it had been crumpled all up together. There are ranch houses in New Spain which make a better appearance at a distance. It is a village of about two hundred warriors, three and four stories high, with the houses small and having only a few rooms, and without a courtyard.[2]

Mota Padilla describes the same village:

> They reached Tribola [another common spelling for Cibola] which was a village divided into two parts [probably similar to presentday Taos Pueblo] encircled in such a way as to make the village round, and the houses adjoining, three and four stories high, with doors opening on a great court or plaza, having one or two doors in the wall so as to go in and out. In the middle of the plaza there is a hatchway or trapdoor by which they go down to a subterranean hall, the roof of which was of large pine beams, and a little hearth in the floor, and the walls plastered.

It is worth noting that when they built in New Mexico the Spanish did not follow the multi-storied forms of the Pueblo Indians but used the traditional house around a court as in Spain.

In describing conditions at Tiguex,[3] Castaneda gives

a very accurate account of how the Indians constructed their adobe walls:

> They worked together to build the villages, the women being engaged in making the mixture and the walls, while the men bring the wood and put it in place. They have no lime, but they make a mixture of ashes, coals and dirt, which is almost as good as mortar, for when the house is to have four stories they do not make the walls more than half a yard thick. They gather a great pile of twigs of thyme and sedge grass and set it afire, and when it is half coals and ashes they throw a quantity of dirt and water on, mixing it all together. They make round balls of this, which they use instead of stone after they are dry, fixing them with the same mixture, which comes to be like a stiff clay.

This description is very interesting, as the ball type adobe can be seen in many walls of buildings still standing in New Mexico. Burning thyme and grass was undoubtedly a folk science that had developed based on scientific fact without scientific understanding. The crude lime ash produced tended to neutralize the acidity of the adobe soil. The acid condition of soils is one of the greatest factors causing erosion, as rainwater running over acid soils tends to form a carbonic acid which dissolves the crystalline binders in the soil. The Bible speaks of the necessity of having manure of the ox to make brick. This too is folk science, as the manure produces a weak ammonia, an acidity neutralizer.

Many descriptions in early Greek and especially Roman literature describe the Mediterranean house as square, with flat roof formed by laying logs across from wall to wall and placing willows or other small woods across the logs. Layers of mud sloping to drains formed from hollow logs were applied over this and allowed to dry. These descriptions often refer to the white plaster walls inside with floors of flat stones or of dried mud swept clean. They are quite typical of the New Mexican house of the seventeenth, eighteenth, and early nineteenth centuries.

According to nineteenth-century descriptions by Zebulon Pike, Josiah Gregg and others, Hispanic New Mexican houses were very similar in character to the Mediterranean house. It was a thick-walled building around one or more inner courts or patios. All rooms opened into the inner court, and quite often there was a porch or portal running around all four court walls.

These houses, or haciendas as they are sometimes called, were built in isolation, usually without any outside openings except a pair of heavy, wooden, gate-like doors large enough to ride horses and pull carts through. Such houses served as a fort in times of raids. In towns, they were built along streets, each house adjoining the next, with the large gate doors opening onto the street. The isolate house with porches or portals to the outside and without courtyard or patio almost certainly did not develop until the towns were secure from raids, probably after the American occupation in the 1840s.

The pre-American house had few windows, usually with a wood grill of simple round poles built into the adobe. Sometimes grills were formed of crudely turned spindles or flat slat types shaped in silhouette. I have heard of and read references to windows covered with a thin parchment (dried skin of animals) or sheets of mica, which is native to northern New Mexico, but I have never seen such and so cannot vouch for them.

Glass windows were so few before the coming of the American trade wagons in 1821 that they are unimportant as an architectural form. The Americans brought the small, paned glass window set in wood sticking known as the "Colonial" window. These were double hung in type, made up of glasses from seven to ten inches wide and from ten to fourteen inches tall, with six, eight, twelve and sixteen lights (glasses) in each sash, and sometimes with nine lights over six, or twelve over eight. With the window sash came Colonial doors and trim similar to that being used in the then young United States.

About this time the first fired bricks were made in New Mexico and the so-called Territorial style developed. This style was often a remodelling job on an older house with brick coping being added and larger windows cut into walls, especially on the street side. The sawmill also came with the Americans, and the outside portal and square post with typical modified Colonial trim was added at this time. The trim applied to the adobe house did not stop with these early forms of the classical Colonial proportions but followed the styles of the eastern part of the United States, where American Gothic "gingerbread" developed in the 1840s to 1870s. These forms were very amusing and interesting when adapted to the adobe by native carpenters with their own feeling for the ornate. Many of the old houses of Los Lunas, below Albuquerque, were still intact in the late 1920s and early 1930s and were quite exciting as architectural expressions of a people adapting a new form to their needs and tastes.

The fireplaces, developed in Spain or somewhere in the Mediterranean area, were generally of the corner type, which is simply a smoke gathering hood above the corneer with a tapering flue through the roof. The taper develops a ventura effect which forms a strong draft as soon as the smoke becomes hot. The fireplace on the flat wall seems to have been a rarity until after the American occupation, when the fireplace began to be trimmed in wood, at first similar to the classical Colonial type. As native craftsmen remodelled the older, corner type, these became quite gay and original in form.

The earliest doors were of the heavy, paneled type with small panels generally raised on one face. They were usually about two to three and a half inches thick, with panels from four inches to about eight or ten inches in width and from six to sixteen inches or more in height. The panels were crudely molded and raised, with the face sometimes carved or otherwise decorated. The rails and sticking were often beaded. Sometimes, but rarely, mitered-in moldings ran around the panels. These doors were generally of the large or small gate type, about two feet wide by about five feet tall.

The sills to the small doors were generally about a foot off the floor. I think this was done to save wood and perhaps to keep down cold floor drafts. Many of these small doors are still intact. They often had the old head and foot peg, or pivot hinge.

About this time another form of door developed— one in which the wood is applied over a core made of tongue and grooved boards. (It is illustrated under the title "Detail, old doors, circa 1850.") These doors are very interesting. I thought they were a local development until I saw similar doors in rural houses in France dating from about the same time. They are still the most expressive forms developed and, when polychromed, the most intriguing of all the door forms.

Some points in the classification of New Mexican architectural styles should be clarified. I have employed terms used rather loosely over a great many years, not because they are the most descriptive or accurate in describing the styles but because they have a common currency.

The "Spanish-Pueblo" is the earliest form, quite common, and probably prevalent in Spain at the time of the settlement of New Mexico. This is a style where the walls are of adobe, usually about two feet thick, although some houses I have seen have had walls thirty- and thirty-six-inches thick. The ratio of thickness is in rela-

tion to the height of the wall. Walls were laid up, gradually reducing the width toward the top to form a battered silhouette. This has sometimes been attributed to erosion over time, but I am more inclined to believe that builders pulled the walls in. Craftsmen rarely used any kind of level and felt that it was better to reduce the load (width) with height to give better stability to the wall.

These walls were usually set in mud mortar on a foundation of rock—ledge type where available, otherwise round field stone. Sometimes this foundation was run up above ground two to three feet and exposed in the finished wall, often even on the interior of the house.

Walls were almost always plastered over with mud (adobe) plaster, and some interesting forms developed. In the northern mountain villages the adobe mud was laced with new, dry, wheat straw which was exposed after the first good rain to produce an intriguing texture. In some areas a clay and small buckshot to pea gravel was used to produce a very rough texture. Walls were rounded over at the top and the line was never level or true. Corners were softened and reveals at openings were sculptured in form.

The floor of the early house was almost always of hardened adobe mud smoothed by hand and kept broom clean. Often these were hardened by painting them with blood from animals, with soot rubbed in to produce a dark, black-brown color. In the early 1930s a number of houses were built with mud floors that had hot linseed oil brushed into them when dry. Several coats of linseed oil were applied to form a hard surface somewhat similar to a very good linoleum. Some houses had flat stone floors. I doubt if there were any wood floors until after 1840 or so, when the first sawmills began to cut timber in the state.

For the roof structure, pine or fir logs were peeled smooth and laid across the walls at about thirty- to thirty-six-inch centers, with the size determined by the span. Across this was laid split native cedar or juniper, small pine poles about two inches in diameter, or small willow stems. A layer of straw was laid over this and then about eighteen to twenty-four inches of adobe mud applied. The surface was almost flat, with just enough slope to drain off water to "canales."

Older houses were apparently laid out by eye without use of square or line. I have worked on many remodelling jobs for houses whose rooms where as much as three feet off a square. This is the general condition rather than the exception. In addition, the house will often have the battered wall of the Spanish-Pueblo type, with the typical Colonial door and window details or even "gingerbread" of the late Victorian period.

This prompts the observation that many of the most interesting examples of New Mexican houses are not of a pure type but a combination of several different styles. The portal or porch of the Spanish-Pueblo style, for example, generally has posts of round pine or fir logs, capped with a wood corbel and square beam, usually hand adzed to shape. There are many fine examples of Spanish-Pueblo houses where a Colonial portal has been added with great charm and interest.

The Territorial style is a combination of several elements. Walls were of adobe with burned brick firewall or coping. These were applied to older houses with the battered walls left and capped only. After American occupation, new adobe walls were usually laid up using a level, so walls are plumb or near plumb, although still from eighteen to twenty-four inches thick. The walls of the Territorial house were generally plastered with a lime-sand stucco which is much better for adobe than the harder cement stucco used today.

Doors and windows were American Colonial (Greek revival) in character or late Victorian "gingerbread." Territorial style doors were usually Colonial, but many fine examples of the old, heavy, paneled Spanish door or the appliqued door can be found. Windows in the Territorial house were generally set to the outside face of the wall with the Colonial trim on the outside (also true of the window when installed in the Spanish-Pueblo house). Inside, the adobe walls were splayed back at an angle and plastered, occasionally with a paneled reveal installed with wood casing on the room side of the wall. Nearly all the windows had a wide wood stool.

The beams of the Territorial houses were often sawmill-cut or adzed, squared beams with sawn or split boards laid over. One of the interesting patterns was to lay the poles and split cedar at an angle to the beam, alternating the direction to form a herringbone pattern.

This was sometimes done with boards stained in pastel colors to form herringbone stripes across the ceiling.

An early house style described in Coronado's journals but rarely built today was the "Jacal." This was a house of cedar posts set in a trench in the ground, edge to edge, with the tops cut off level at plate height. A vee-ed beam was placed as a collar, with the typical viga, or beam, construction over. The posts were plastered or chinked between with adobe mud; the inside face was generally plastered over to form a smooth surface and painted white.

The burned clay tile roof, so typical of modern Spain and Mexico and of Spanish settlers in California, was not found in New Mexico before about 1880. Again, I think this is due to the background of the early colonists, who came from rural Spain where the tile roof was not extensively used at that time. When the earth roof was found to serve fairly well to protect the house from rain and snow, no effort was made to deevelop kilns to burn the clay tile. California, on the other hand, was settled much later by more affluent settlers who were familiar with then current Spanish and Mexican architecture.

NOTES

1. The quotations are from *The Journey of Coronado*, translated and edited by George Winship Parker (New York: A. S. Barnes, 1904).

2. In referring to the courtyard, Castaneda probably has in mind the Mediterranean type plan around four sides of a patio.

3. Tiguex, west of presentday Bernalillo, was excavated by the Museum of New Mexico under a Works Progress Administration project in the mid-1930s. It is now maintained as part of the Museum of New Mexico system and is open to the public.

DRAWINGS

On the following pages are floor plans, elevations or perspectives, and details of the elements of houses modeled on an older house or a combination of houses. In most cases I have modified the design to conform to contemporary living patterns.

These drawings are presented to help both the long-time resident and the newcomer to the Southwest identify and appreciate the various forms of adobe architecture found here. The plans do not propose to be studies from which houses can be built. The home planner should consult his local licensed architect for professional help. The architect is an expert on these matters who is familiar with local conditions and will make an effort to discover your needs and budget and to design a house to meet these demands. Remember: Not even the wealthy can afford to build without the services of an architect.

PERSPECTIVE

del Patio House: In the historical introduction to this book I have written about the typical Spanish house built around a patio. This early house is still one of the most practical for the Southwestern climate. This small house, with the open porch or bridge type portal forming one side of the patio, will let a breeze flow through the patio and keep it cool during the summer months. The form of this house is one that the architect can take and develop into many variations.

Generally a two-car garage is almost a necessity in today's American society. This basic plan can easily be expanded to include the garage, just as other areas can be expanded for more room. The garage door shown is a built-up type similar to the doors hereinafter illustrated.

The patio side of the portal could be closed in to form a private patio if desirable. This should be done with advice from your local architect, who will know what is best for your family pattern and the climate of your locale. In the arid Southwest, a shallow pool in the patio adds interest and acts as a cooling agent during the summer months.

del · PATIO ·

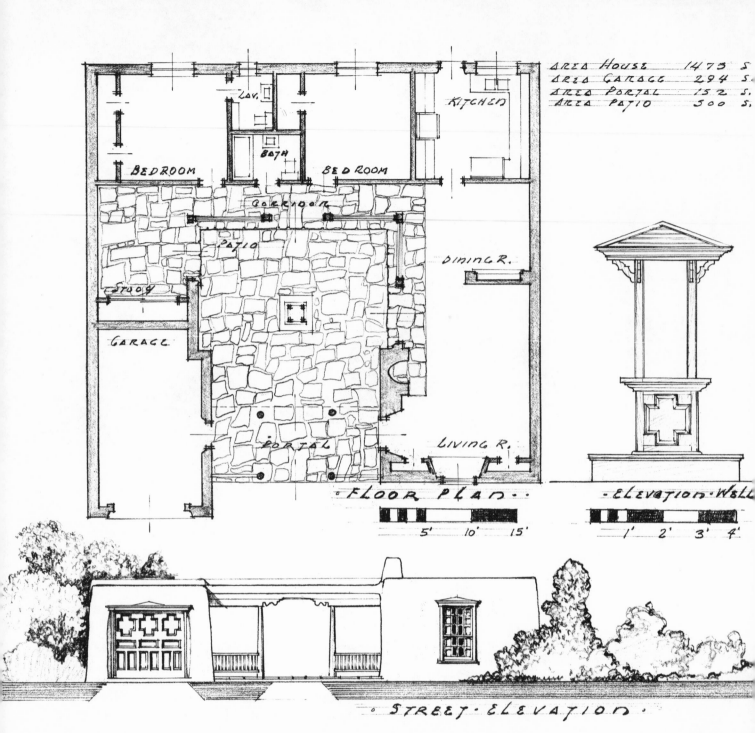

AREA HOUSE   1475 S.
AREA GARAGE   294 S.
AREA PORTAL   152 S.
AREA PATIO   500 S.

KITCHEN

LAV.

BATH

BEDROOM   BEDROOM

BEDROOM

PATIO

DINING R.

STUDY

GARAGE

PORTAL

LIVING R.

·FLOOR·PLAN·

·ELEVATION·WELL·

5'   10'   15'

1'   2'   3'   4'

·STREET·ELEVATION·

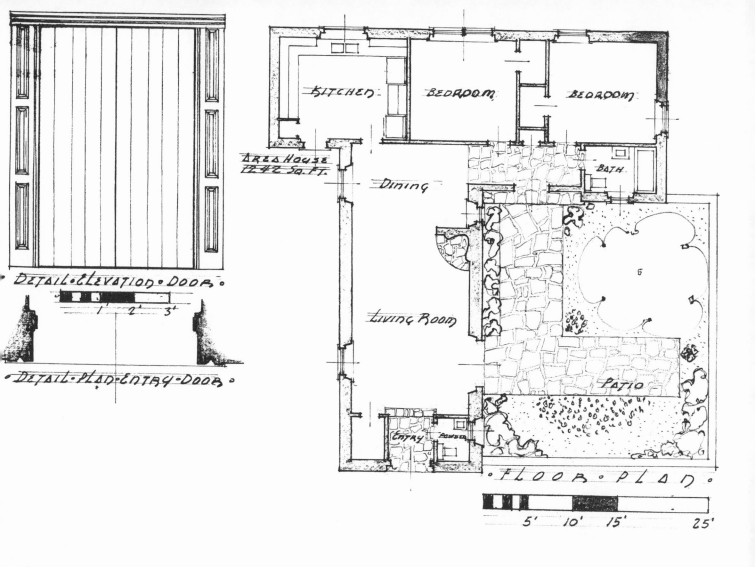

· DETAIL · ELEVATION · DOOR ·

· DETAIL · PLAN · ENTRY · DOOR ·

1 2 3

AREA HOUSE
1242 SQ. FT.

KITCHEN

BEDROOM

BEDROOM

BATH

DINING

LIVING ROOM

PATIO

ENTRY

POWDER

· FLOOR · PLAN ·

5' 10' 15' 25'

FRONT · ELEVATION

Alcalde

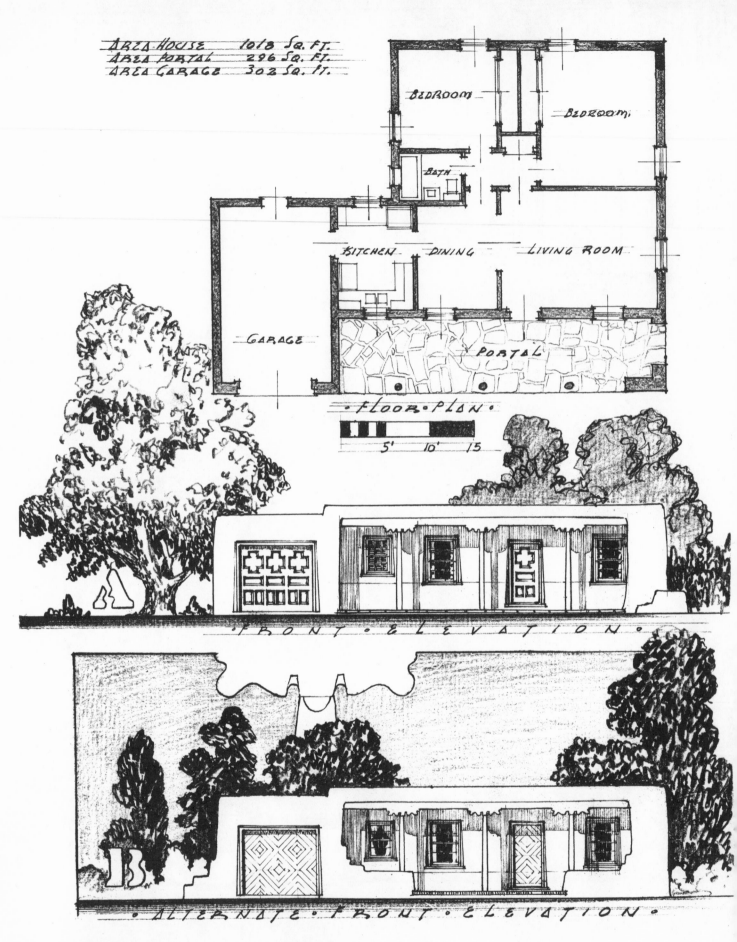

AREA HOUSE   1018 SQ. FT.
AREA PORTAL   296 SQ. FT.
AREA GARAGE   302 SQ. FT.

BEDROOM

BEDROOM

BATH

KITCHEN   DINING   LIVING ROOM

GARAGE

PORTAL

· FLOOR · PLAN ·

5'   10'   15

· FRONT · ELEVATION ·

· ALTERNATE · FRONT · ELEVATION ·

Abiquiu House

AREA HOUSE   1275 SQ. FT.
AREA GARAGE   360 SQ. FT.
AREA PORTAL   123 SQ. FT.

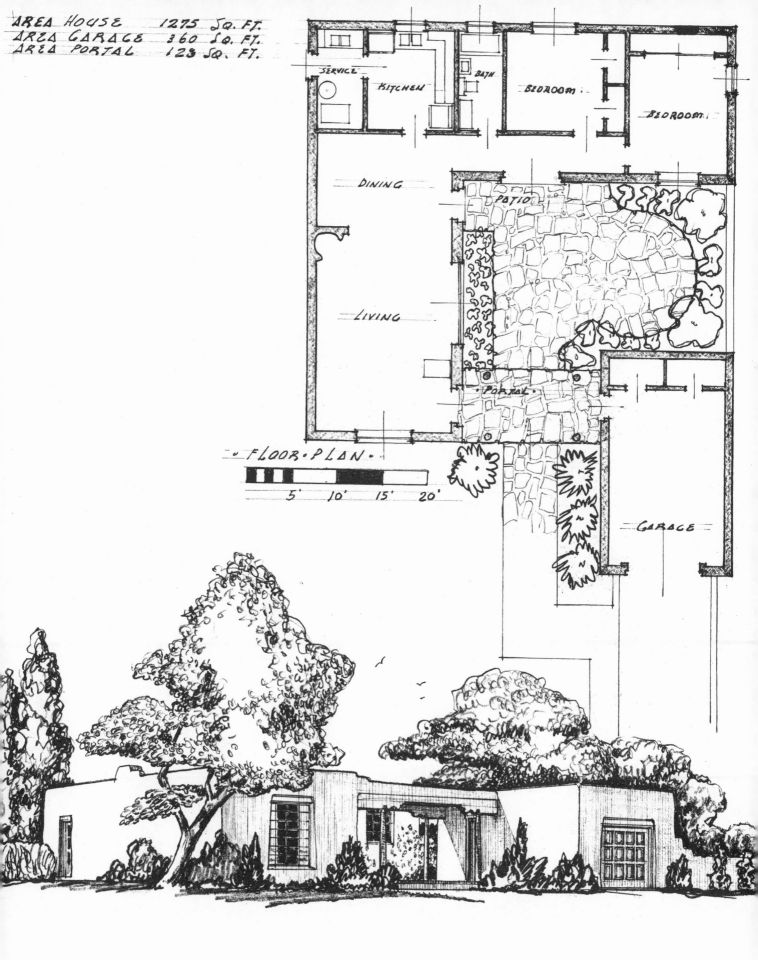

SERVICE   KITCHEN   BATH   BEDROOM   BEDROOM

DINING

PATIO

LIVING

PORTAL

·FLOOR·PLAN·

5'   10'   15'   20'

GARAGE

El Patio

11

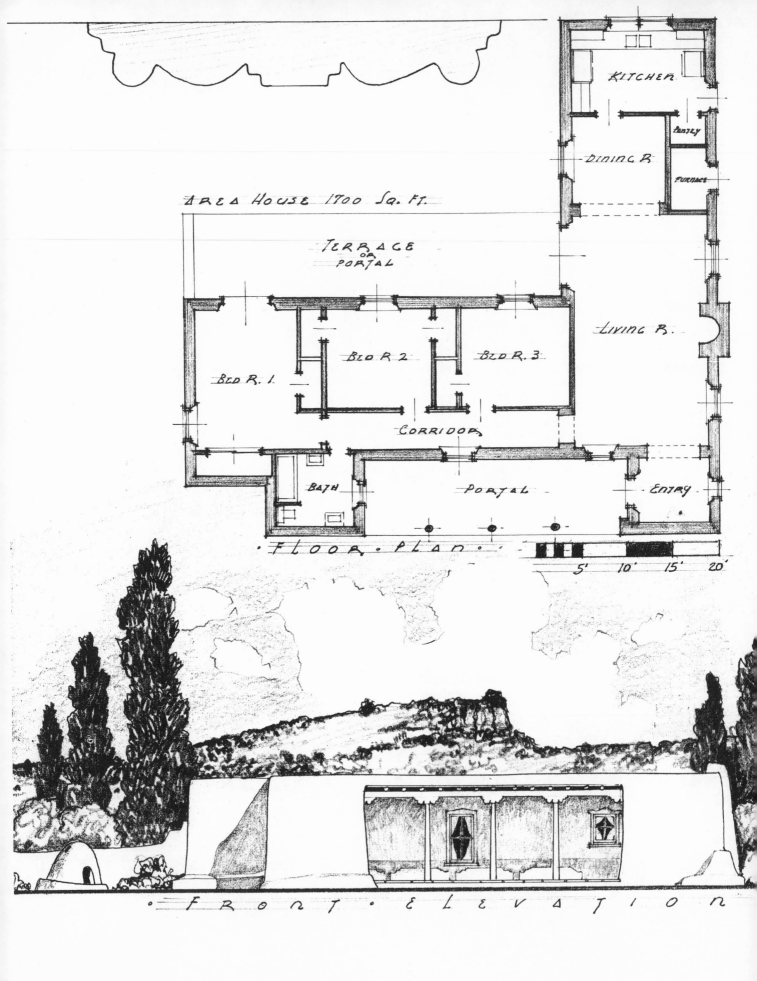

AREA HOUSE 1700 Sq. Ft.

KITCHEN

DINING R.

PANTRY

FURNACE

TERRACE OR PORTAL

LIVING R.

BED R. 1

BED R. 2

BED R. 3

CORRIDOR

BATH

PORTAL

ENTRY

· Floor · Plan ·

5'   10'   15'   20'

· Front · Elevation ·

Casa · del · Campo

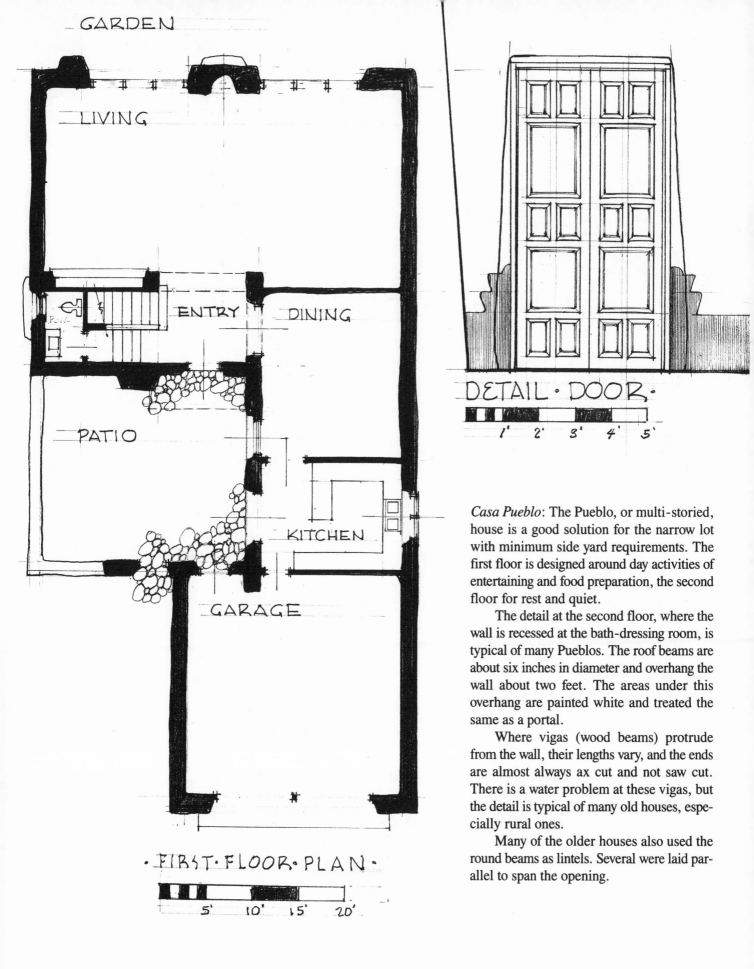

GARDEN

LIVING

ENTRY DINING

PATIO

KITCHEN

GARAGE

· FIRST · FLOOR · PLAN ·

5' 10' 15' 20'

DETAIL · DOOR ·

1' 2' 3' 4' 5'

Casa Pueblo: The Pueblo, or multi-storied, house is a good solution for the narrow lot with minimum side yard requirements. The first floor is designed around day activities of entertaining and food preparation, the second floor for rest and quiet.

The detail at the second floor, where the wall is recessed at the bath-dressing room, is typical of many Pueblos. The roof beams are about six inches in diameter and overhang the wall about two feet. The areas under this overhang are painted white and treated the same as a portal.

Where vigas (wood beams) protrude from the wall, their lengths vary, and the ends are almost always ax cut and not saw cut. There is a water problem at these vigas, but the detail is typical of many old houses, especially rural ones.

Many of the older houses also used the round beams as lintels. Several were laid parallel to span the opening.

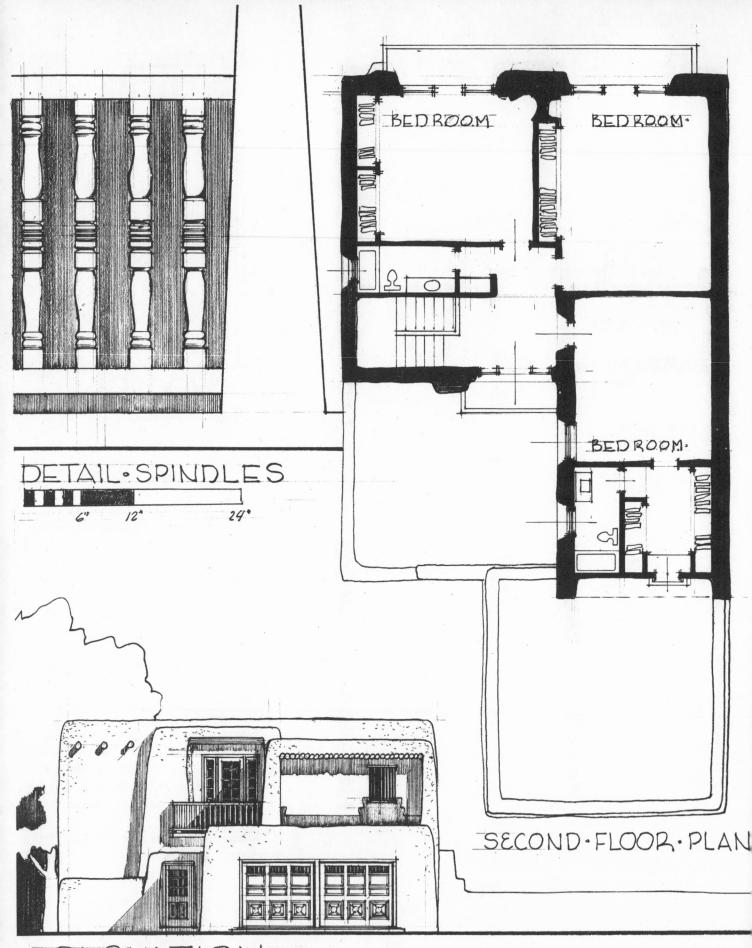

DETAIL·SPINDLES

6" 12" 24"

BEDROOM

BEDROOM

BEDROOM.

SECOND·FLOOR·PLAN

ELEVATION·

PERSPECTIVE

La Plazuela: Due to archaic setback and side yard requirements, land used for residential purposes in the average American town is tragic in its waste. Numerous articles and books have been written on this land waste, but nothing has been done. The real problem should be attacked by citizens and architects to change land use zoning laws and to allow for the development of the patio house—a much more intelligent form—especially in the Southwest.

Studies of this situation can be secured by anyone interested. With the cost of land development skyrocketing to where the neighborhood home builder has to charge his customer roughly forty to fifty percent of the selling cost of the house as the land, selling, improvement and other non-

building costs, a better utilization of land is paramount. With side yard requirements eliminated, the forty-foot lot might even be desirable and could save several thousand dollars on the cost of the finished house.

The Plazuela house is presented as a possible solution to circumvent side yard requirements. The house could be set at the usual side yard offset with no openings along this wall. Each house in a given block could be arranged so that a use deed might be executed to give the neighbor the use of the side yard area as patio and outdoor living development. This is only an expedient, not the final solution, however.

La Plazuela

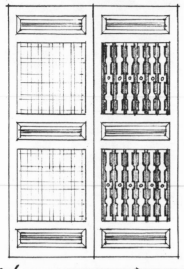

· ELEVATION · DOORS ·

12"   2'   3'   5'

· ELEVATION · STREET · WINDOWS ·

REQUIREMENTS LOT · 50' x 100'
FACING NORTH OR WEST

AREA HOUSE	1146 S.F.
AREA GARAGE	370 S.F.
AREA TERRACE	400 S.F.
COVERED ENTRY	150 S.F.

PLAN ·· A

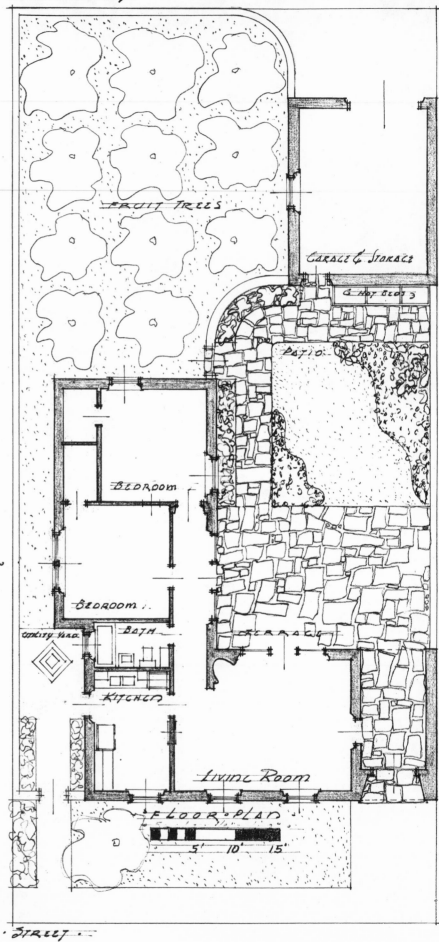

PUBLIC ALLEY

FRUIT TREES

GARAGE & STORAGE

G HOT BEDS

PATIO

BEDROOM

BEDROOM ·

UTILITY YARD

BATH

TERRACE

KITCHEN

LIVING ROOM

· FLOOR · PLAN ·

5'   10'   15'

· STREET ·

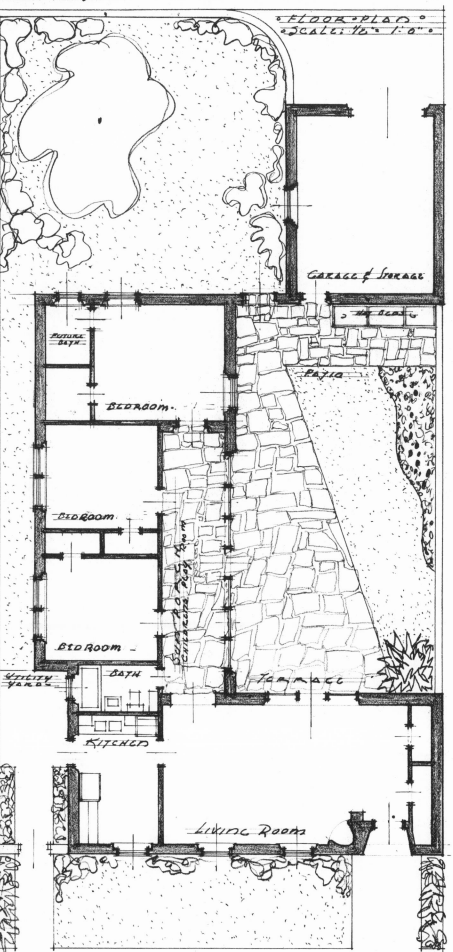

° FLOOR · PLAN °
° SCALE: 1/2" = 1'·0" °

GARAGE & STORAGE

PATIO

FUTURE BATH

BEDROOM

BEDROOM

CHILDRENS PLAY or PLAYROOM

BEDROOM

BATH

TERRACE

UTILITY YARD

KITCHEN

LIVING ROOM

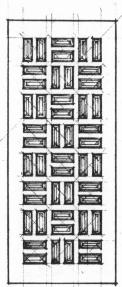

· ELEVATION · FRONT · DOOR ·

1'   2'   3'   4'

HOUSE AREA	1640 S.F.
GARAGE AREA	370 S.F.
TERRACE AREA	534 S.F.
LOT REQUIRED	50'·0" x 100'·0"

PLAN ⋀⋀⋀ B

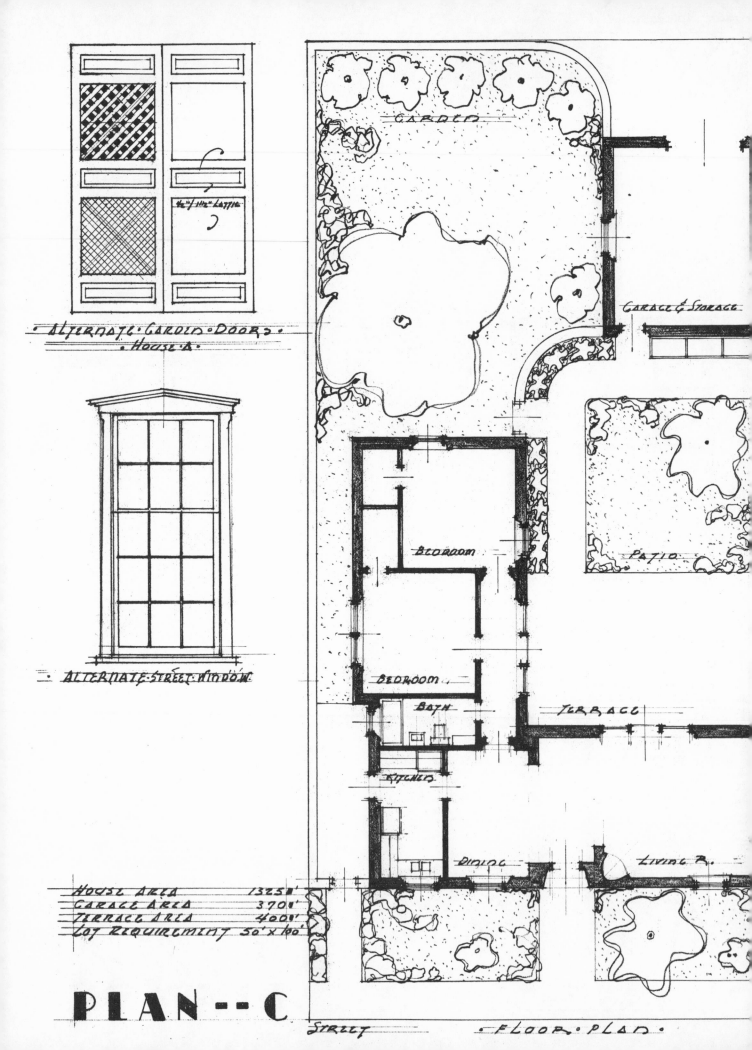

· ALTERNATE · GARDEN · DOORS ·
· HOUSE · A ·

½" / 1½" LATTICE

GARDEN

GARAGE & STORAGE

PATIO

· ALTERNATE · STREET · WINDOW ·

BEDROOM

BEDROOM

BATH

TERRACE

KITCHEN

HOUSE AREA   1325☐'
GARAGE AREA   370☐'
TERRACE AREA   400☐'
LOT REQUIREMENT 50'x100'

DINING

LIVING R.

PLAN -- C

STREET   · FLOOR · PLAN ·

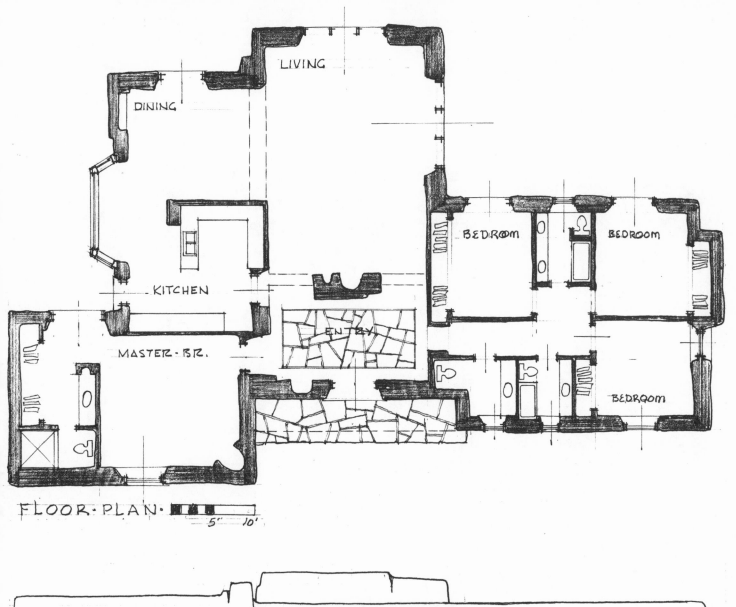

DINING

LIVING

BEDROOM

BEDROOM

KITCHEN

ENTRY

MASTER·BR.

BEDROOM

FLOOR·PLAN·

5' 10'

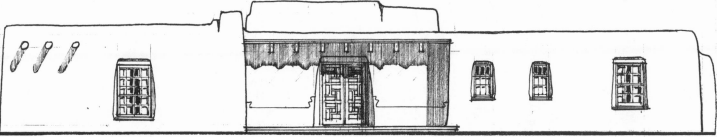

·ELEVATION·

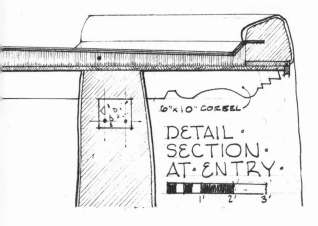

6"x10" CORBEL

DETAIL·
SECTION·
AT·ENTRY·

1' 2' 3'

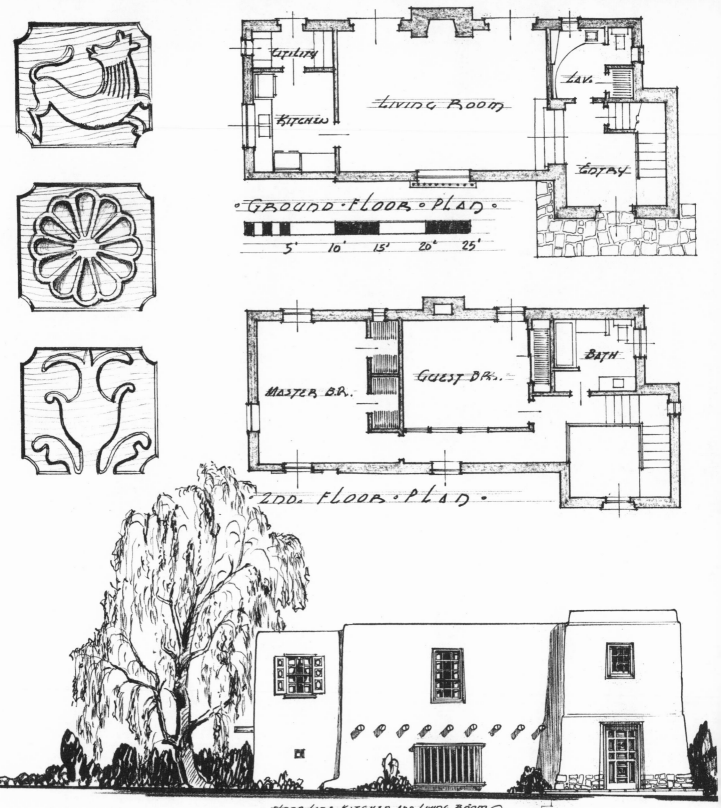

· GROUND · FLOOR · PLAN ·

Living Room

Utility

Kitchen

Lav.

Entry

5'   10'   15'   20'   25'

· 2nd. · FLOOR · PLAN ·

Master B.R.

Guest BR.

Bath

FLOOR LINE KITCHEN AND LIVING ROOM

· FRONT · ELEVATION ·

AREA	GROUND FLOOR	649 SQ. FT.
AREA	SECOND FLOOR	649 SQ. FT.
AREA	ENTRY HALL	196 SQ. FT.
	TOTAL	1494 SQ. FT.

El Torreón

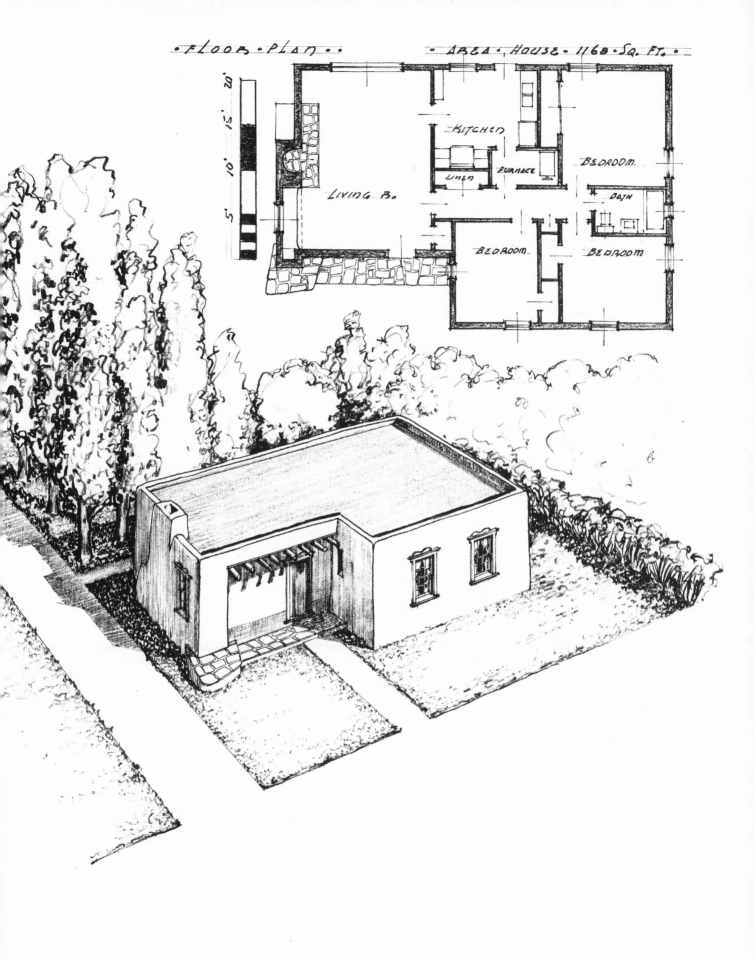

·FLOOR·PLAN·· ·AREA·HOUSE·1168·SQ·FT·

KITCHEN

LINEN FURNACE

BEDROOM

LIVING R.

BATH

BEDROOM BEDROOM

El·Amarillo·

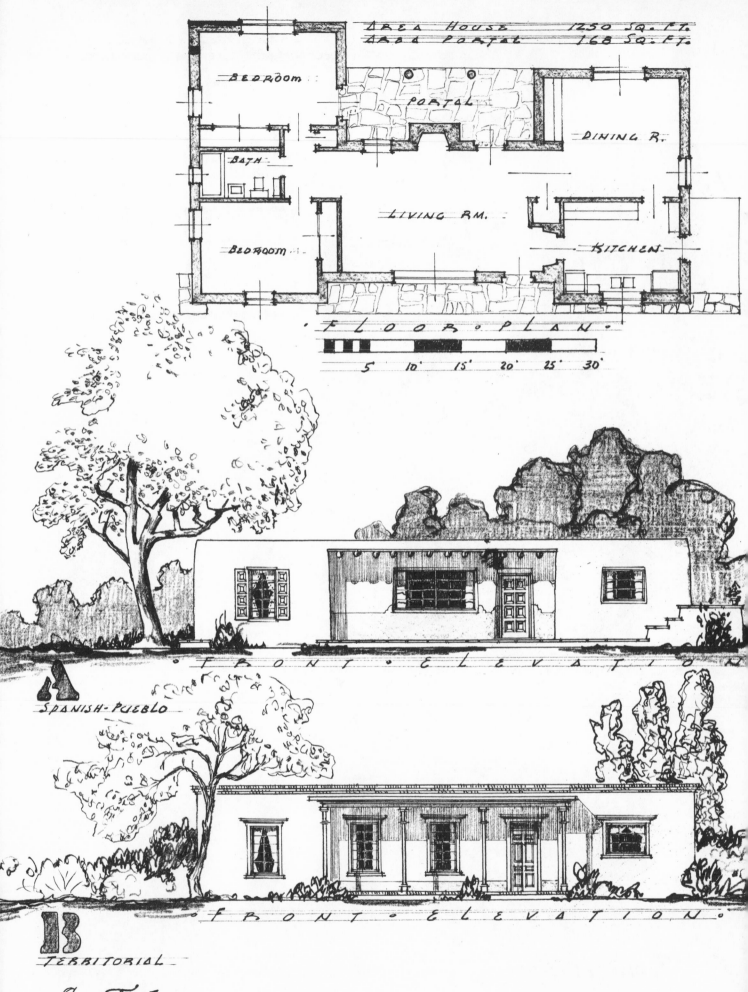

AREA HOUSE   1250 SQ. FT.
AREA PORTAL   168 SQ. FT.

BEDROOM

PORTAL

DINING R.

BATH

LIVING RM.

BEDROOM

KITCHEN

· FLOOR · PLAN ·

5   10'   15'   20'   25'   30'

· FRONT · ELEVATION ·

A SPANISH-PUEBLO

· FRONT · ELEVATION ·

B TERRITORIAL

La Talpa

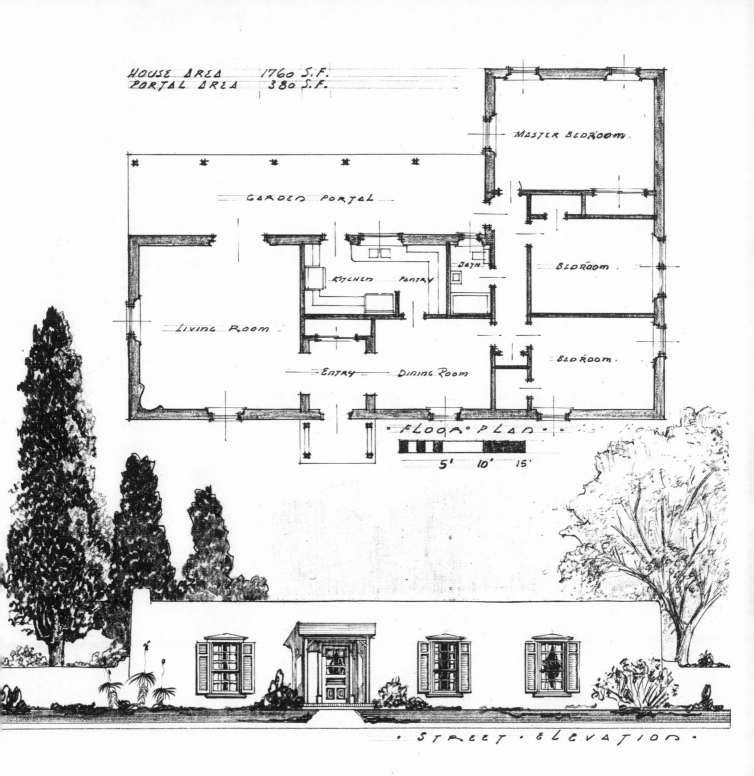

HOUSE AREA   1760 S.F.
PORTAL AREA   380 S.F.

GARDEN PORTAL

MASTER BEDROOM

LIVING ROOM

KITCHEN   PANTRY   BATH

BEDROOM

BEDROOM

ENTRY   DINING ROOM

· FLOOR · PLAN ·

5'   10'   15'

· STREET · ELEVATION ·

Camino Cañon

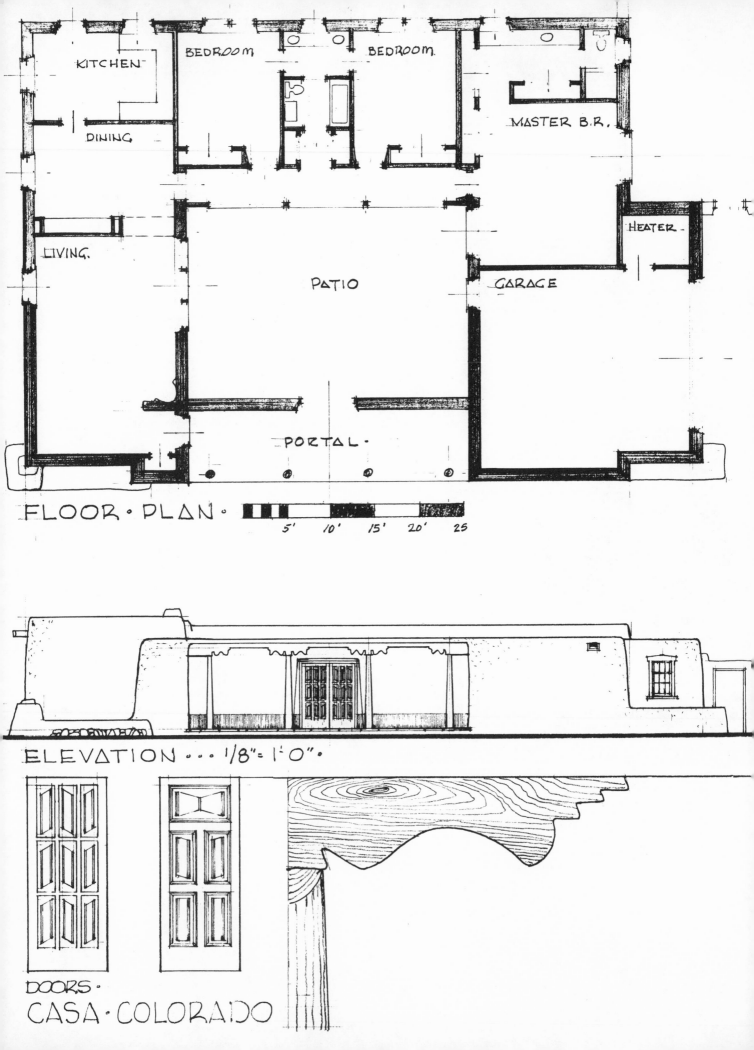

KITCHEN

BEDROOM

BEDROOM.

MASTER B.R.

DINING

HEATER

LIVING.

PATIO

GARAGE

PORTAL.

FLOOR · PLAN ·

5'   10'   15'   20'   25

ELEVATION ... 1/8" = 1'·0"·

DOORS·

CASA · COLORADO

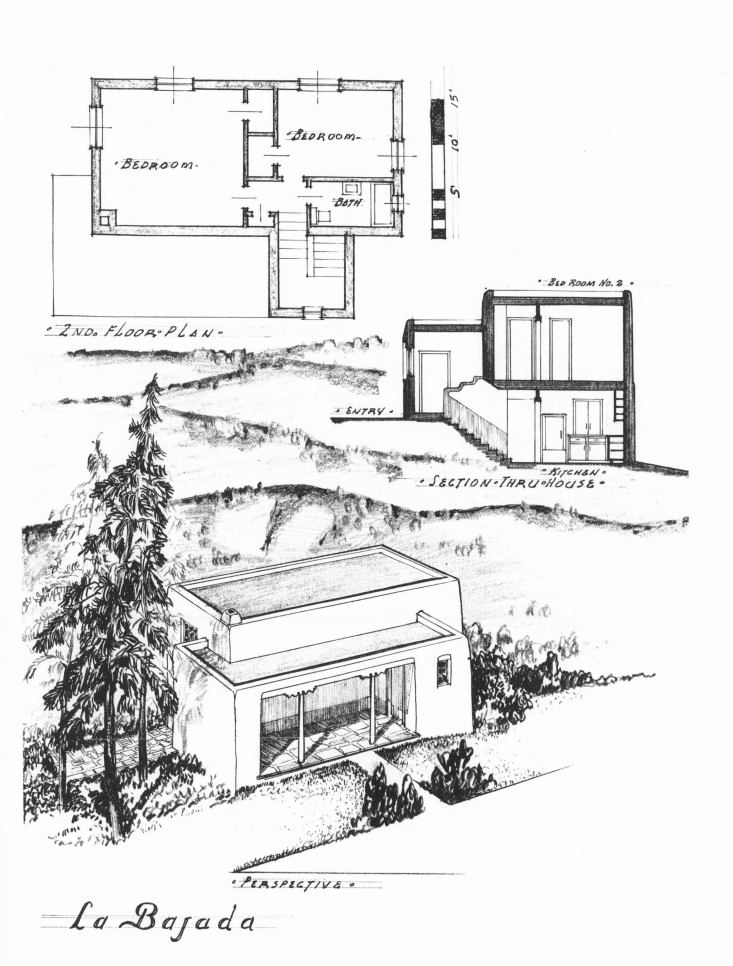

·2ND·FLOOR·PLAN·

·BEDROOM·

·BEDROOM-

·BATH·

5'   10'   15'

·BED ROOM No. 2·

·ENTRY·

·KITCHEN·

·SECTION·THRU·HOUSE·

·PERSPECTIVE·

La Bajada

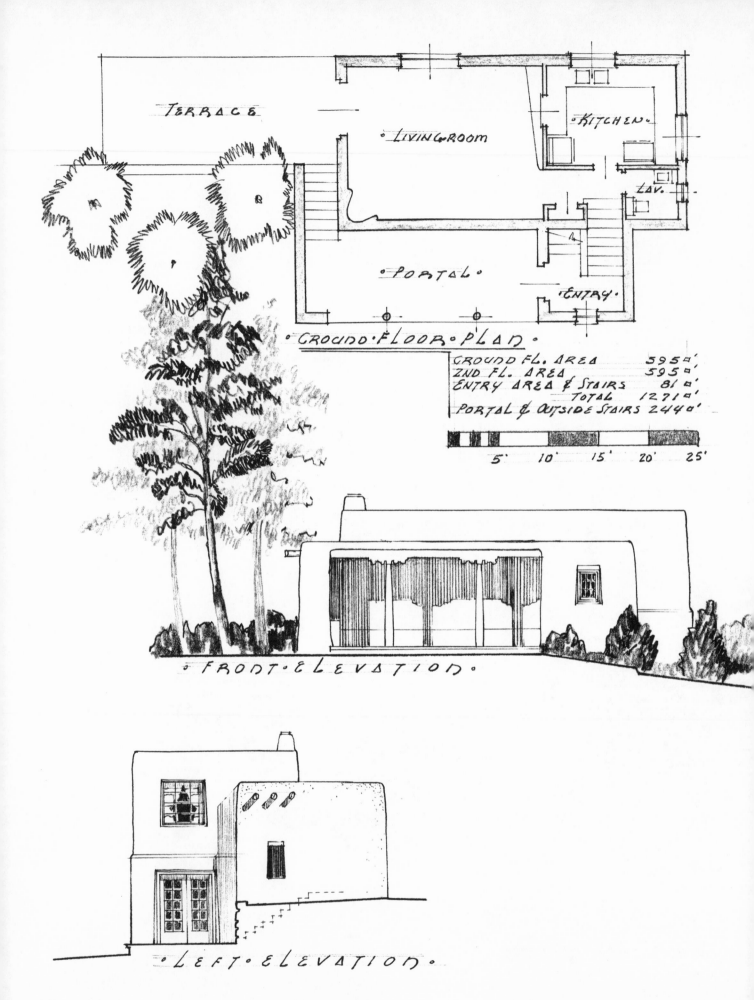

TERRACE

LIVINGROOM

KITCHEN

LAV.

PORTAL

ENTRY

·GROUND·FLOOR·PLAN·

GROUND FL. AREA	595▫'
2ND FL. AREA	595▫'
ENTRY AREA & STAIRS	81▫'
TOTAL	1271▫'
PORTAL & OUTSIDE STAIRS	244▫'

5'   10'   15'   20'   25'

·FRONT·ELEVATION·

·LEFT·ELEVATION·

AREA HOUSE 1160 SQ. FT.
AREA PORTAL 320 SQ. FT.

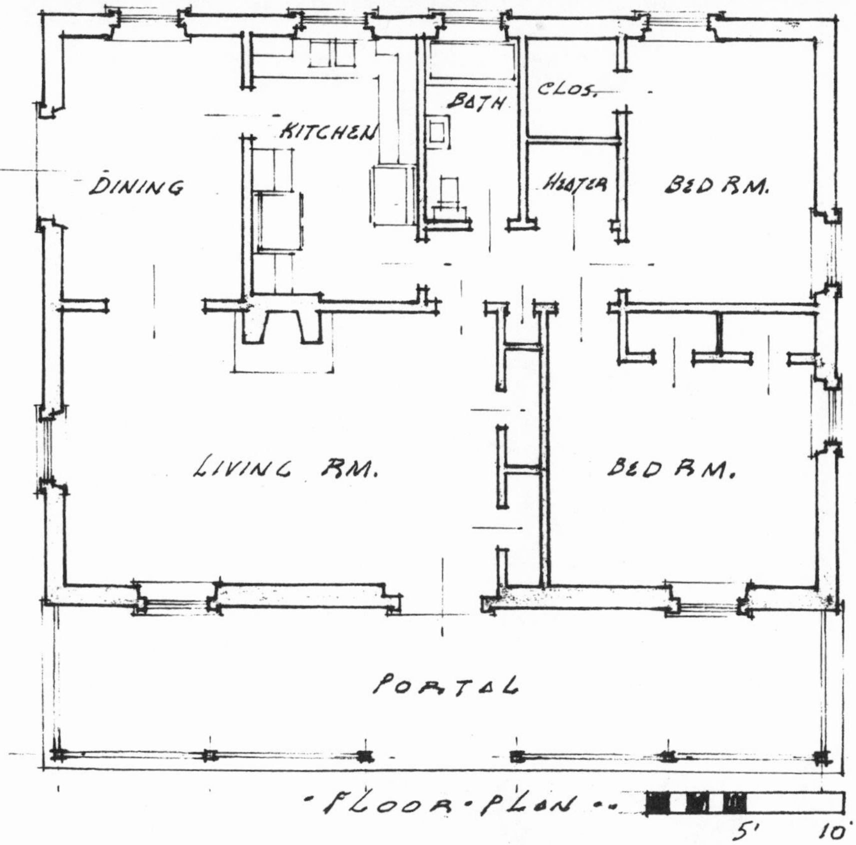

DINING

KITCHEN

BATH   CLOS.

HEATER   BED RM.

LIVING RM.

BED RM.

PORTAL

·FLOOR·PLAN··

5'   10'

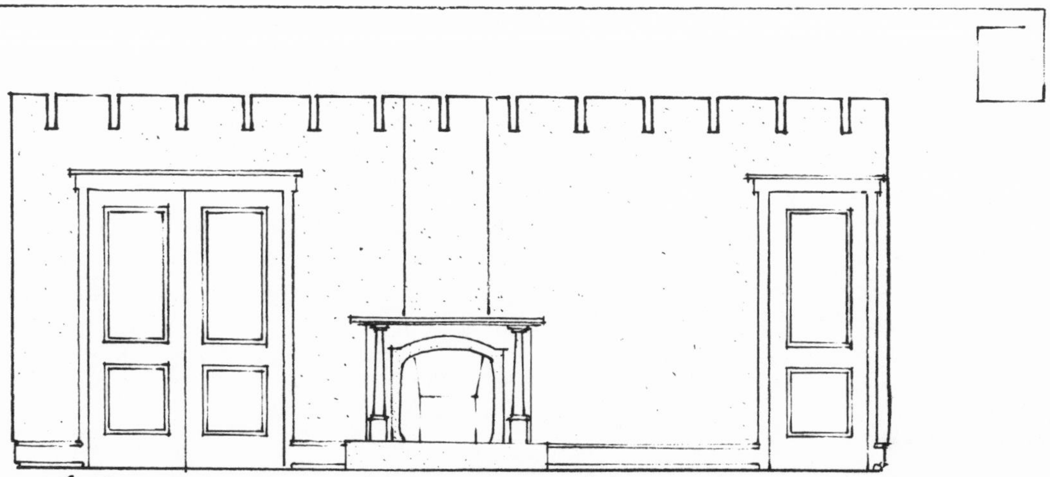

·ELEVATION·LIVING·R.··

·The·Borrego·House·

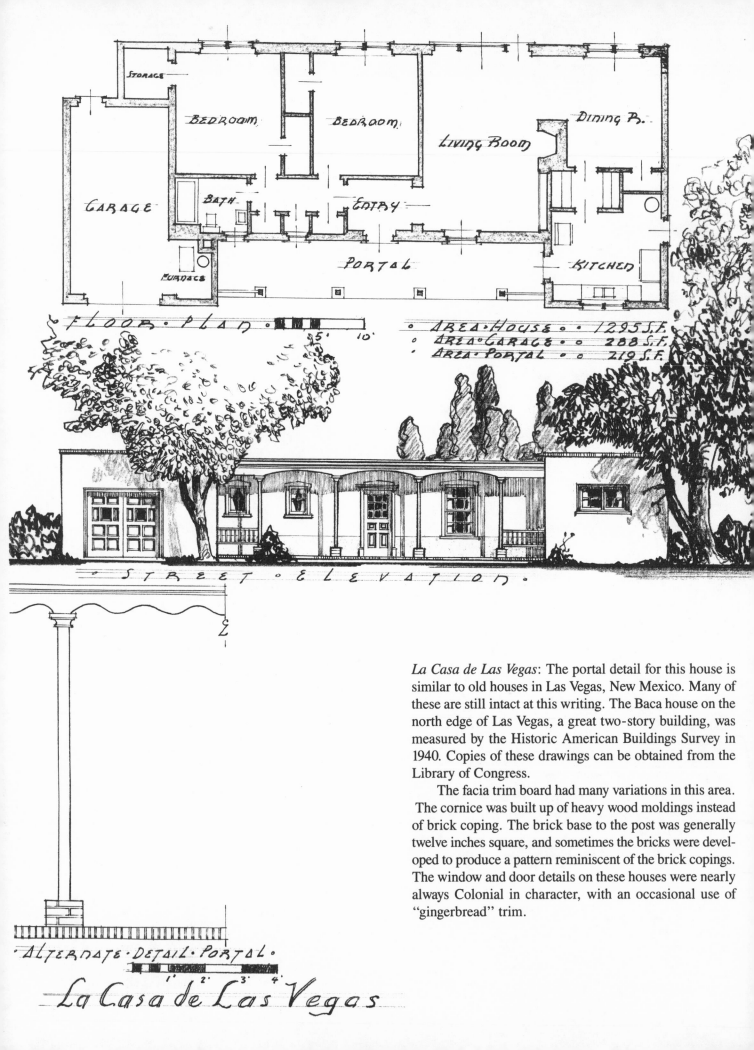

STORAGE

BEDROOM   BEDROOM   Living Room   DINING R.

GARAGE   BATH   ENTRY   KITCHEN

FURNACE   PORTAL

FLOOR PLAN   5'   10'

AREA HOUSE   1295 S.F.
AREA GARAGE   288 S.F.
AREA PORTAL   219 S.F.

STREET ELEVATION

ALTERNATE DETAIL PORTAL   1'   2'   3'   4'

La Casa de Las Vegas

La Casa de Las Vegas: The portal detail for this house is similar to old houses in Las Vegas, New Mexico. Many of these are still intact at this writing. The Baca house on the north edge of Las Vegas, a great two-story building, was measured by the Historic American Buildings Survey in 1940. Copies of these drawings can be obtained from the Library of Congress.

The facia trim board had many variations in this area. The cornice was built up of heavy wood moldings instead of brick coping. The brick base to the post was generally twelve inches square, and sometimes the bricks were developed to produce a pattern reminiscent of the brick copings. The window and door details on these houses were nearly always Colonial in character, with an occasional use of "gingerbread" trim.

BEDROOM   BEDROOM   BEDROOM   MASTER B.R.

PATIO

PATIO RM.

UTILITY

LIVING RM.

GARAGE

ENTRY   DINING.   KITCHEN

PORTAL

FLOOR · PLAN · ·

5'   10'   15'   20'

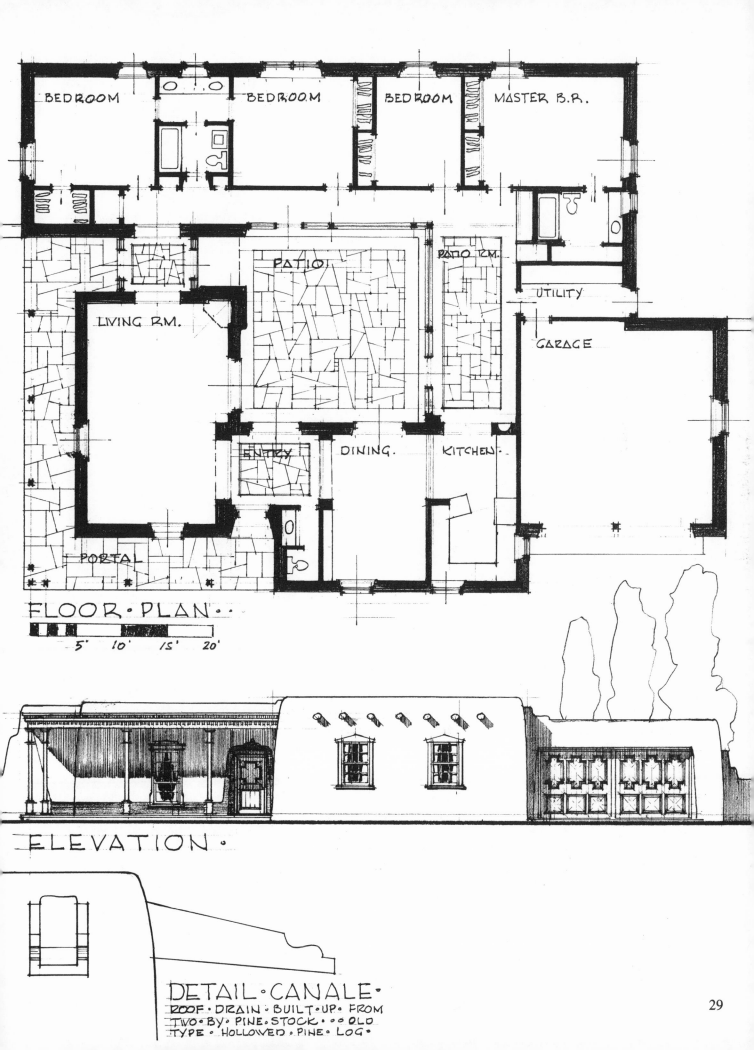

ELEVATION ·

DETAIL · CANALE ·
ROOF · DRAIN · BUILT · UP · FROM
TWO · BY · PINE · STOCK · ·· OLD
TYPE · HOLLOWED · PINE · LOG ·

29

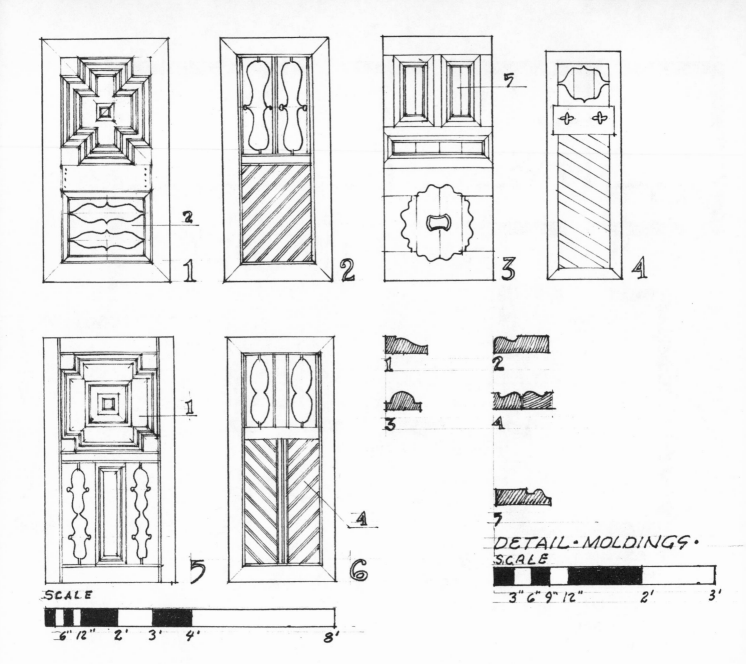

DETAIL·MOLDINGS·
SCALE
3" 6" 9" 12"   2'   3'

SCALE
6" 12"   2'   3'   4'   8'

Detail Old Doors, Circa 1850: I have dated these doors as around 1850 because most of them were made using cut nails which were a product of the eastern United States at this time and were probably brought out by wagon in the trade caravans. Secondly, all the surviving examples are made of mill sawn lumber, and the sawmill was not introduced into New Mexico until 1840 or later.

The patterns were rich in form, and many original types were developed. Historically, I am not sure where the pattern for these doors originated. I have mentioned seeing similar doors of this period in France and suspect they were also used in Spain. Some of the pattern of paneling is borrowed from the other paneled door. The bandsaw flowing line pattern sometimes seems to be original in the Southwest. The old moldings were always rather shallow in contour, being all hand run with block molding planes.

The construction is simple: The face was applied to a background of 1" x 6" or 8" tongue and grooved material. In old doors the face material was thoroughly nailed to the base, but modern carpenters usually glue the facing on and secure it with wood screws. The development of excellent grades of exterior type playwoods makes it possible to use a sheet of this cut to the door size and apply trim to both faces. These make excellent doors.

detail·old·doors··circa·1850·····

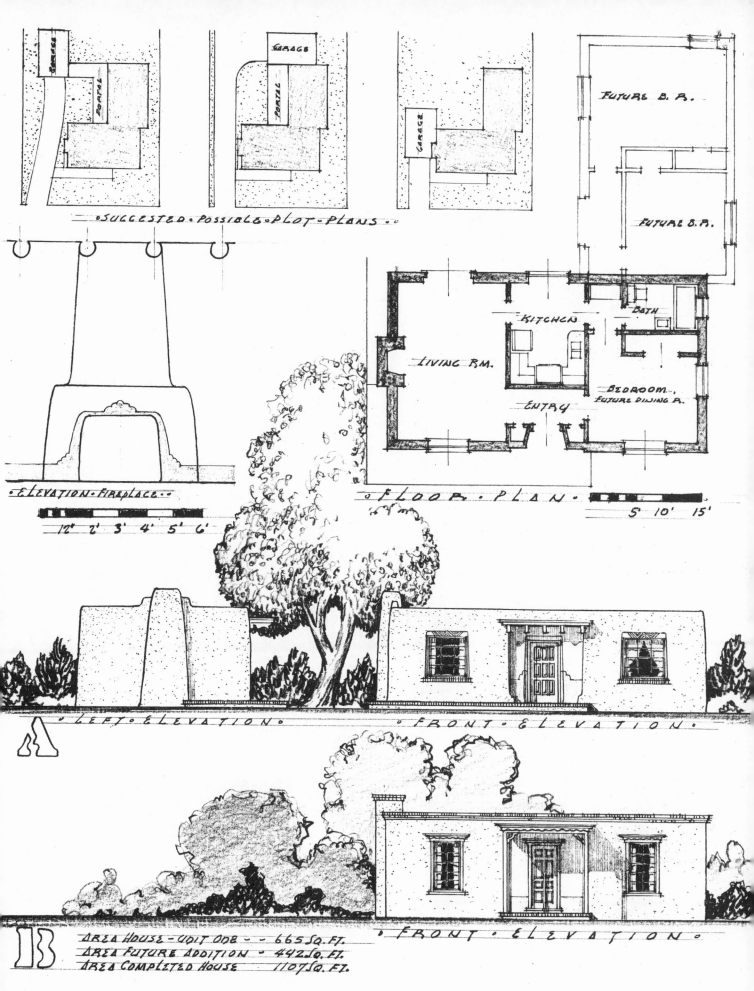

· SUGGESTED · POSSIBLE · PLOT · PLANS ·

GARAGE
PORTAL

GARAGE
PORTAL

GARAGE

FUTURE B.R.

FUTURE B.R.

· ELEVATION · FIREPLACE ·

12" 2' 3' 4' 5' 6'

· FLOOR · PLAN ·

5' 10' 15'

KITCHEN   BATH

LIVING RM.

BEDROOM,
FUTURE DINING R.

ENTRY

· LEFT · ELEVATION ·   · FRONT · ELEVATION ·

· FRONT · ELEVATION ·

AREA HOUSE - UNIT ONE - - 665 SQ. FT.
AREA FUTURE ADDITION - 442 SQ. FT.
AREA COMPLETED HOUSE   1107 SQ. FT.

Dos Casitas

31

Floor·Plan   5'   10'   15

BEDROOM

BEDROOM

BATH

LIVING ROOM   KITCHEN

A   ·FRONT·ELEVATION·

B   FRONT·ELEVATION·   CAR PORT

HOUSE AREA   900 SQ. FT.

Casa de San Ysidro

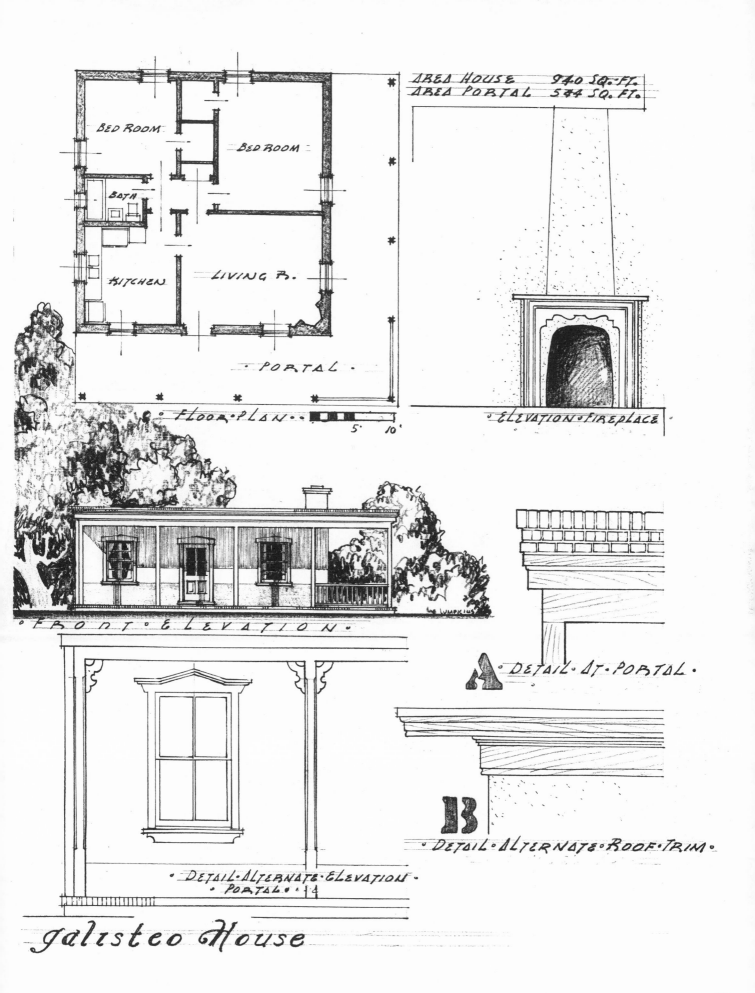

BED ROOM

BED ROOM

BATH

KITCHEN

LIVING R.

· PORTAL ·

· FLOOR · PLAN ··   5'   10'

AREA HOUSE   940 SQ. FT.
AREA PORTAL   574 SQ. FT.

· ELEVATION · FIREPLACE ·

· FRONT · ELEVATION ·

LUMPKINS

A · DETAIL · AT · PORTAL ·

B · DETAIL · ALTERNATE · ROOF · TRIM ·

· DETAIL · ALTERNATE · ELEVATION ·
· PORTAL · A ·

galisteo House

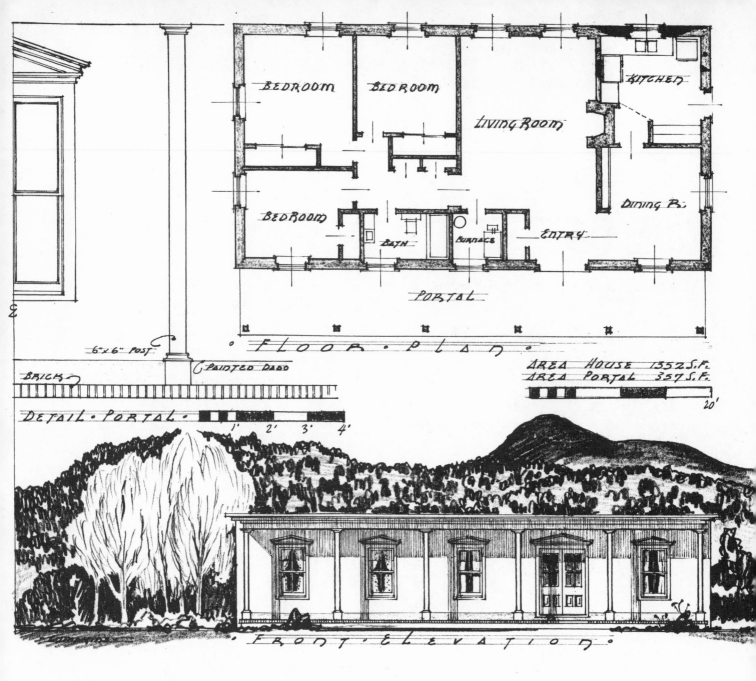

BEDROOM BEDROOM

KITCHEN

LIVING ROOM

DINING R.

BEDROOM

BATH FURNACE ENTRY

PORTAL

FLOOR PLAN

AREA HOUSE 1352 S.F.
AREA PORTAL 357 S.F.

6"x6" POST

BRICK PAINTED DADO

DETAIL PORTAL 1' 2' 3' 4'

20'

FRONT ELEVATION

Puerto de Luna House: This old house existed at Puerto de Luna, a small village south of Las Vegas, New Mexico. Vernon Hunter lived and worked in this house before he became director of the Federal Art Project for New Mexico in the late 1930s.

The detail on this house was very late Colonial, with the large four light windows so typical about 1840 to 1860. The original house was much larger in plan than I have shown it here, where I have scaled down the size to meet the needs of today's family. The original house had a large center hall about ten feet wide running through the house with rooms opening off each side. This was typical of many houses of the period from 1840 to 1890.

At Galisteo, New Mexico, in the late 1920s and early 1930s there were many houses reminiscent of this one. There, the portal often ran all the way around the house to give wall protection from the weather on all four faces of the building. This form could be developed for the house set in a garden or as a method for encouraging outdoor living from all rooms of the house.

In the 1940s I completed several Santa Fe houses in which this portal was developed on at least two sides of the house as "porch-living" areas.

Puerto de Luna

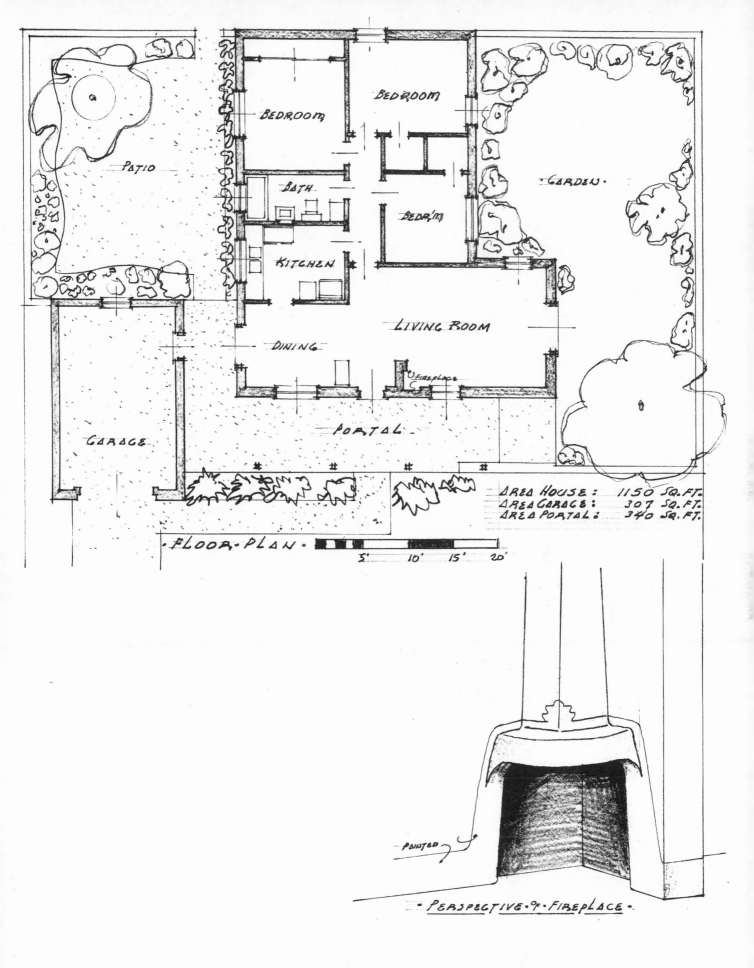

PATIO

BEDROOM

BEDROOM

BATH

BEDR'M

GARDEN

KITCHEN

LIVING ROOM

DINING

Fireplace

GARAGE

PORTAL

AREA HOUSE: 1150 SQ.FT.
AREA GARAGE: 307 SQ.FT.
AREA PORTAL: 340 SQ.FT.

·FLOOR·PLAN·

5'   10'   15'   20'

PAINTED

·PERSPECTIVE·of·FIREPLACE·

La Casa de la Jardine.

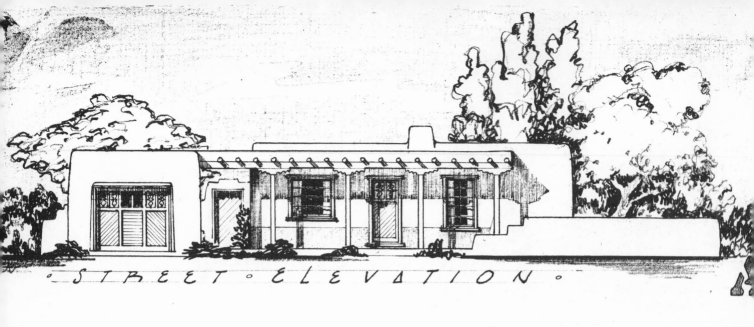

· STREET · ELEVATION ·

STREET · ELEVATION ·

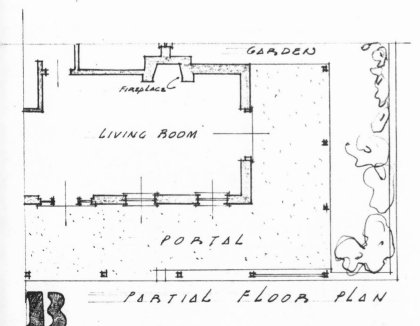

GARDEN

Fireplace

LIVING ROOM

PORTAL

PARTIAL FLOOR PLAN

B

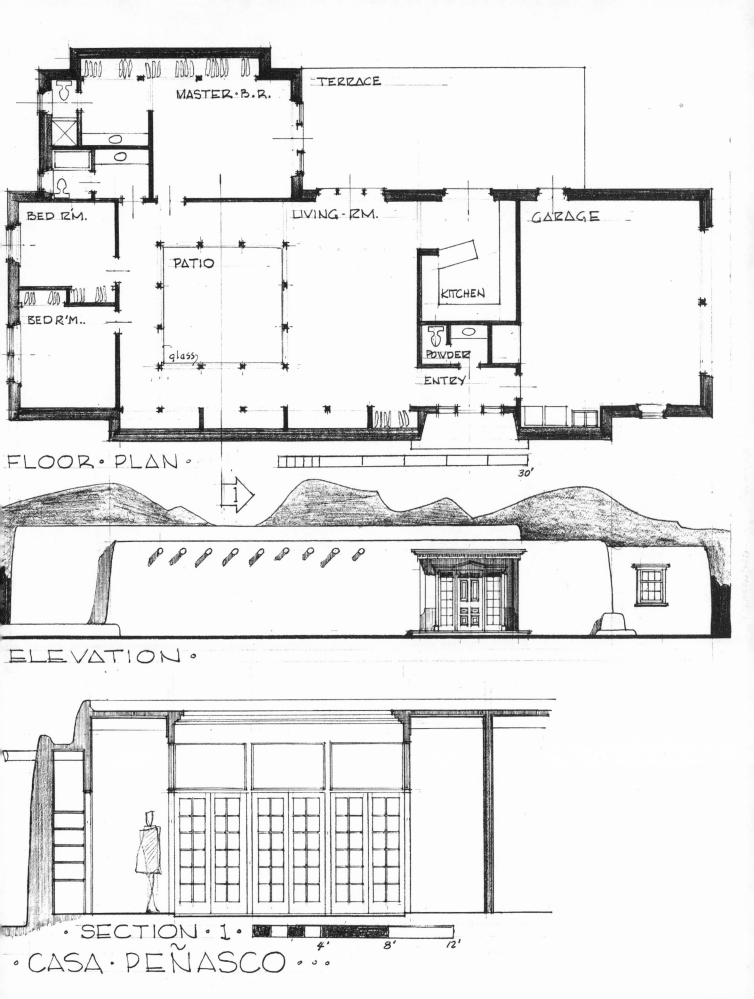

FLOOR · PLAN ·

TERRACE

MASTER · B · R ·

BED RM.

BED R'M..

PATIO

glass

LIVING · RM.

KITCHEN

POWDER

ENTRY

GARAGE

30'

ELEVATION ·

· SECTION · 1 ·
· CASA · PEÑASCO · ° °

4'   8'   12'

37

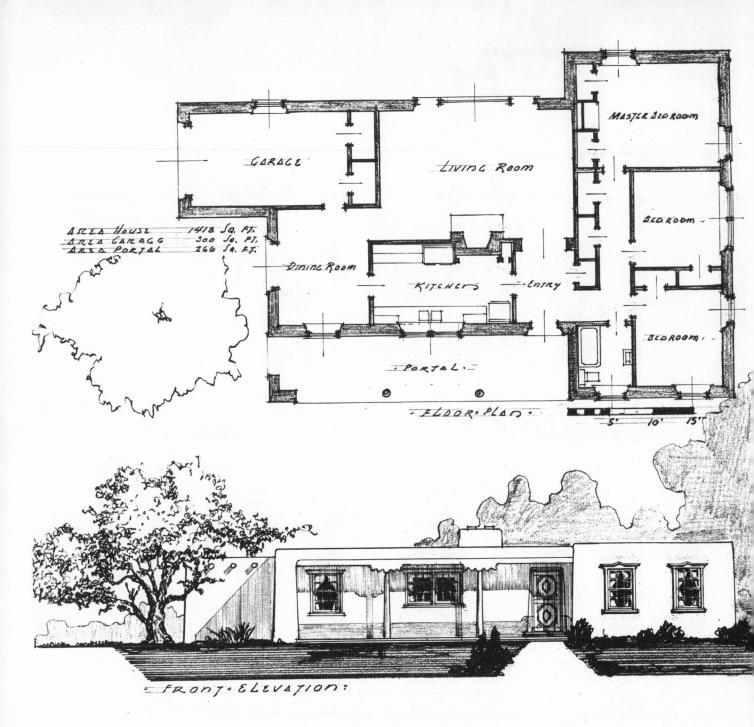

GARAGE

LIVING ROOM

MASTER BEDROOM

BEDROOM

AREA HOUSE 1418 Sq. Ft.
AREA GARAGE 300 Sq. Ft.
AREA PORTAL 266 Sq. Ft.

DINING ROOM

KITCHEN — ENTRY

BEDROOM

PORTAL

FLOOR PLAN

5' 10' 15'

FRONT ELEVATION

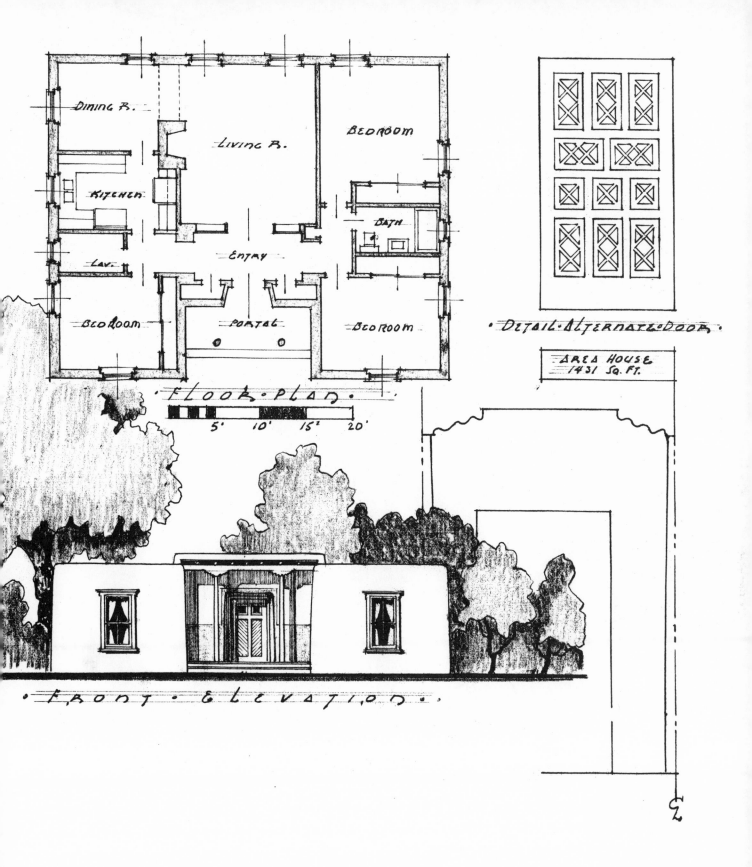

DINING R.

LIVING R.

BEDROOM

KITCHEN

BATH

LAV.

ENTRY

BEDROOM

PORTAL

BEDROOM

· FLOOR · PLAN ·

5'   10'   15'   20'

· DETAIL · ALTERNATE · DOOR ·

AREA HOUSE
1431 SQ. FT.

· FRONT · ELEVATION ·

Los · Griegos ·

SOLAR HOUSE DRAWINGS

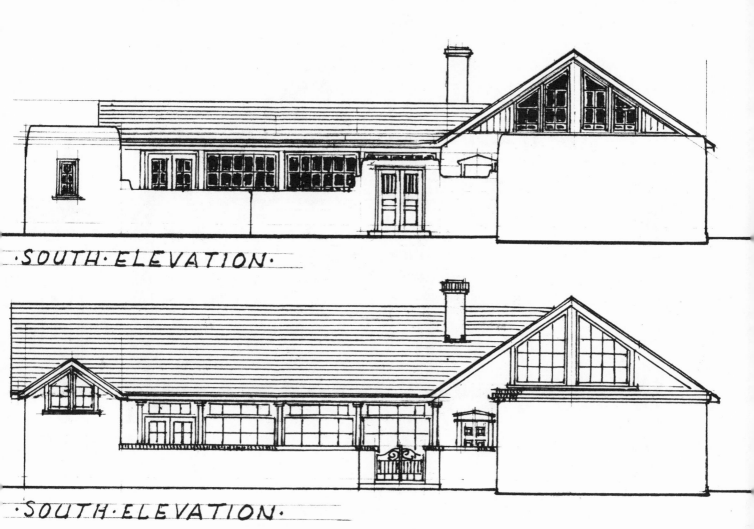

·SOUTH·ELEVATION·

·SOUTH·ELEVATION·

Casa del Norte Solar House: This house, particularly the all-sloping roof version, is for northern New Mexico, Arizona, and southern Colorado. The style is modified northern New Mexican adobe that came into vogue with the coming of the railroads in the early 1880s. Although Zebulon Pike describes a few pitched roofs in 1806-7, this modification occurred after roofing materials like shingles and sheet metal were shipped in from the industrial East.

The plan shows the kitchen and garage wing extending south along the east side. In siting the house it should be tilted some twenty to thirty degrees to the east in order to have the sun penetrate the sun porch as early as possible on winter days. The gable clerestory above the flat roof of the kitchen will charge the wet wall of the living room and the half wall between the living and the dining spaces.

The elevations show two roof framing systems. The top drawing shows the living and dining room having the pitch roof with a pitch only over the sun porch. All other roofs are flat. The lower drawing shows the all-pitch roof.

The detail of the trombe wall shows the use of the wood sticking sash. This modifies the typical wall of this type where only large single sheets are used. Here the storage mass is shown as twelve-inch-thick concrete blocks with all cells filled with concrete. Adobe could be used. Even though not south facing, the trombe wall along the dressing-bath wing should store ample heat for the low volume space.

·CASA·del·NORTE·

43

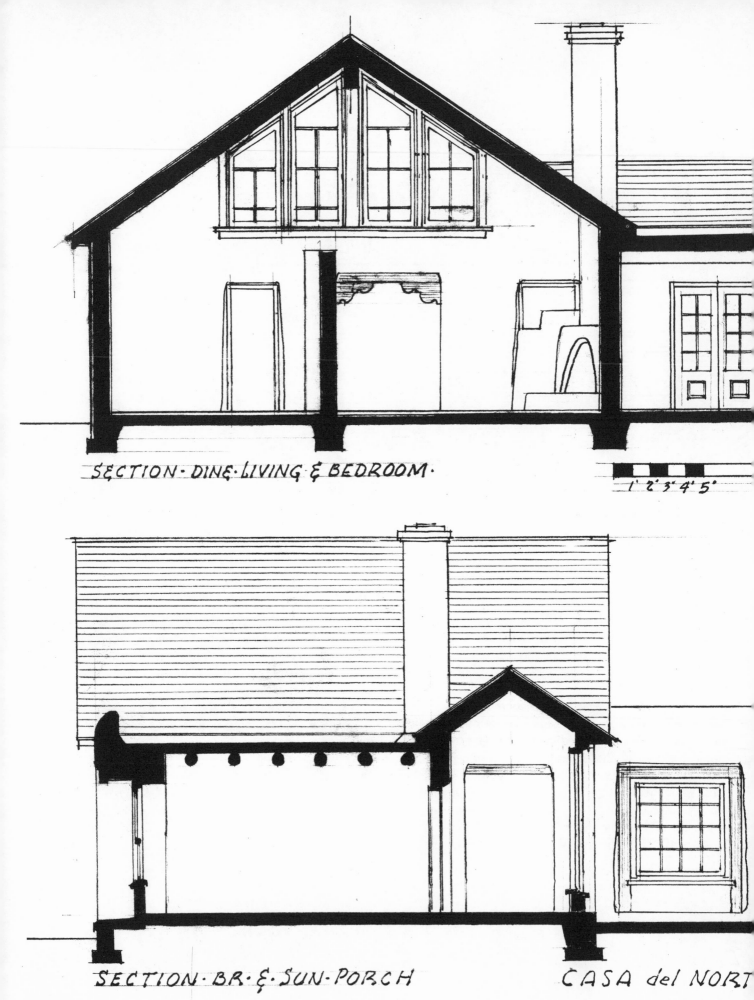

SECTION · DINE · LIVING & BEDROOM ·

1' 2' 3' 4' 5'

SECTION · BR · & · SUN · PORCH

CASA del NORT

44

trombe' wall

SECTION·SUNPORCH·&·BEDROOM·2·

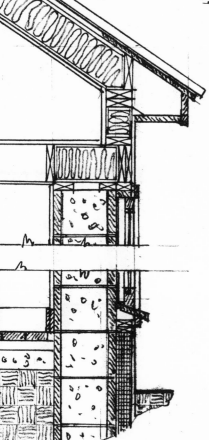

DETAIL·SECTION·TROMBÉ·WALL

CASA del NORTE

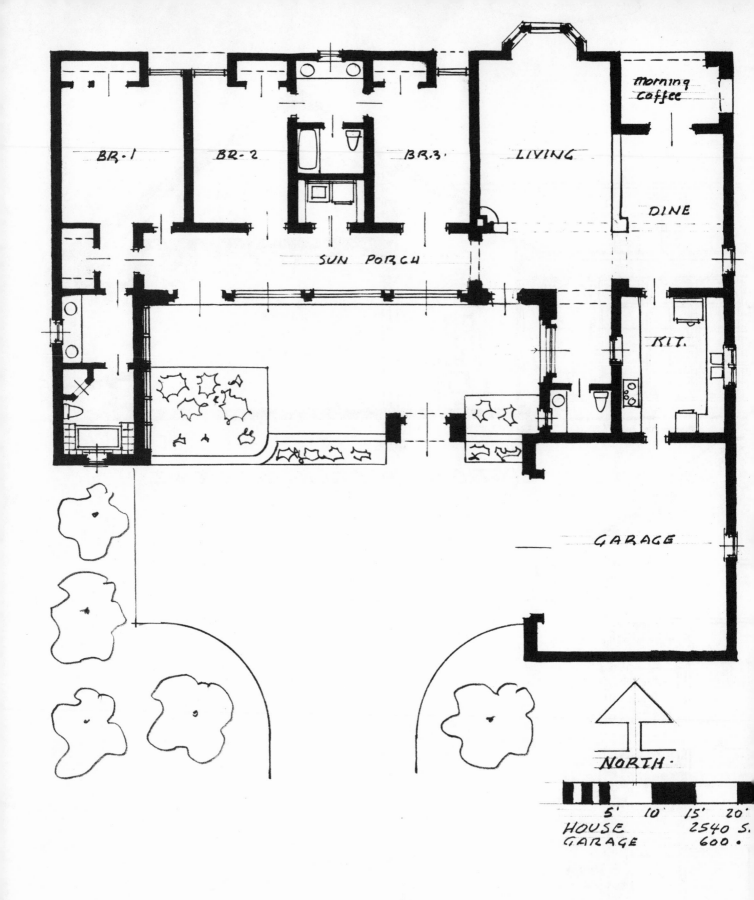

BR·1

BR·2

BR·3

LIVING

morning
coffee

DINE

SUN PORCH

KIT.

GARAGE

NORTH·

5' 10' 15' 20'

HOUSE 2540 S.
GARAGE 600·

·CASA·del·NORTE·

·FLOOR·PLAN·

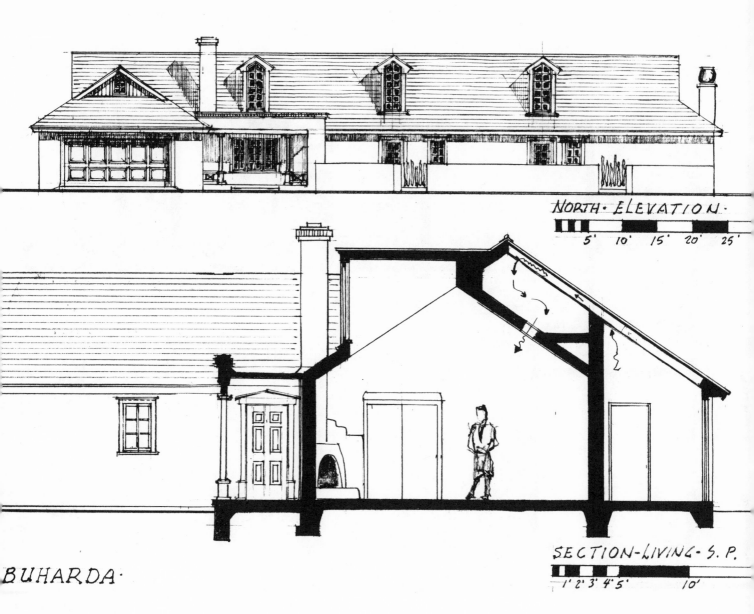

NORTH·ELEVATION·

5'   10'   15'   20'   25'

SECTION-LIVING-S.P.

1' 2' 3' 4' 5'   10'

BUHARDA·

Buharda (Dormer Window) Solar House: The style of this house is reminiscent of the early ranch house of northern New Mexico, although it has its kin on the great windswept plains of America.

The solar system is a sun porch with two components for providing warmth to the living spaces. The sun porch stores heat in the mass wall and by thermal lift forces warm air up through a plenum into an attic chamber where it cools slightly and drops down into the living space. This system should work well where days are sunny but the air is cold. The warm air in the living space would be a welcome note when one entered from the cold outside.

47

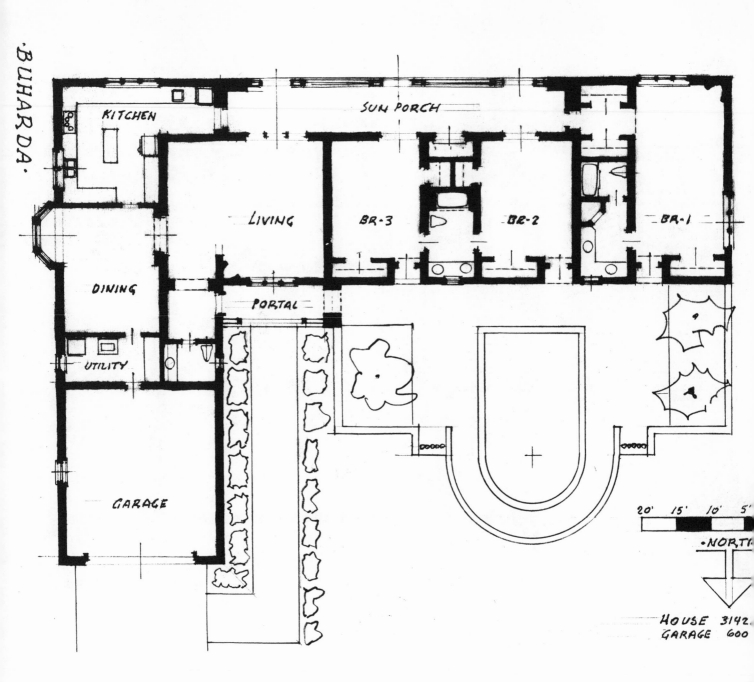

·BUHARDA·

KITCHEN

SUN PORCH

LIVING   BR·3   BR·2   BR·1

DINING

PORTAL

UTILITY

GARAGE

20'   15'   10'   5'

·NORTH·

HOUSE 3142
GARAGE 600

48

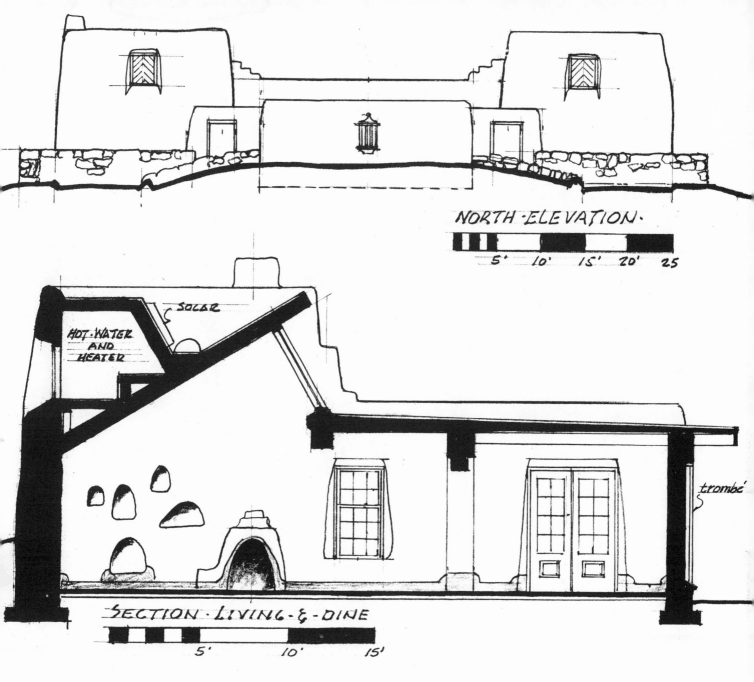

NORTH·ELEVATION·

5' 10' 15' 20' 25

SOLAR

HOT·WATER
AND
HEATER

trombe

SECTION·LIVING·&·DINE

5'   10'   15'

Rincon Solar House: This plan is designed using direct gain and a south facing trombe wall for heating the masses. The direct gain uses two clerestories—one over the living room and the other over bedroom one. The overhang of the roof above the trombe wall is necessary to prevent overheating the mass from May through October. This overhang is designed for the degrees of latitude north or south of the equator. Your architect has tables to determine this.

The design of the massive thirty-inch-thick walls around the north end of the living room and bedroom one create a mass for many hours of heat storage and provide a massive sculptural form for the two volumes. Above the sloping roof is space in an attic for the hot water tank with a reverse stop used to mount the solar hot water collectors.

The drive-through garage saves on backing out into traffic, and, although two overhead garage doors are required, the cost of the second will probably easily save a bent fender. The garage is detached with easy access to the entry gallery across the patio. The position of the garage provides complete privacy for the patio.

RINCÓN·

49

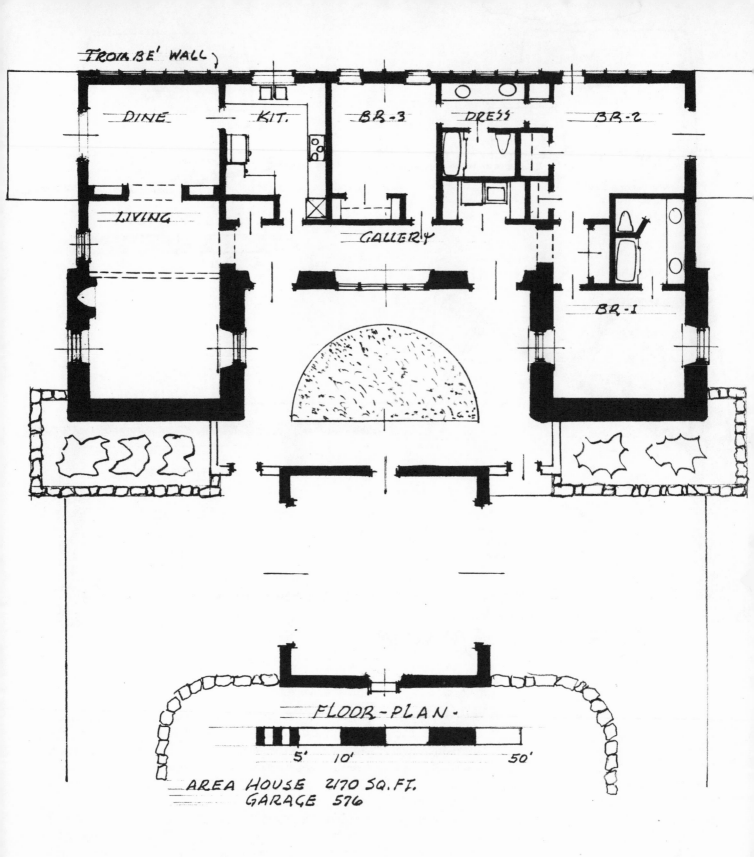

TROMBE' WALL

DINE   KIT.   BR-3   DRESS   BR-2

LIVING

GALLERY

BR-1

FLOOR-PLAN

5'   10'   50'

AREA HOUSE 2170 SQ. FT.
GARAGE 576

·RINCÓN·

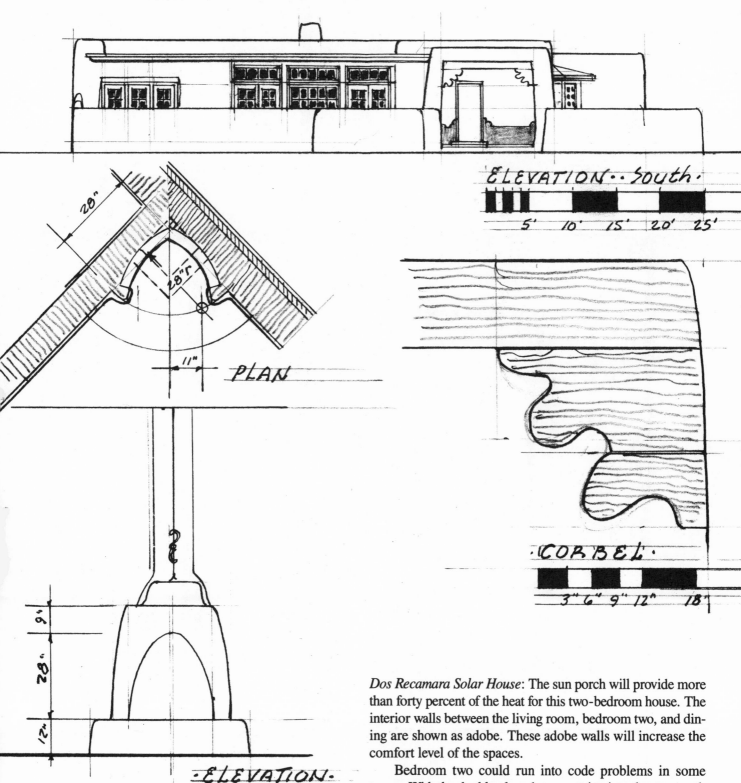

ELEVATION··SOUTH·

5'   10'   15'   20'   25'

·PLAN·

·CORBEL·

3" 6" 9" 12"   18"

·ELEVATION·
·DETAILS·FIREPLACE·

Dos Recamara Solar House: The sun porch will provide more than forty percent of the heat for this two-bedroom house. The interior walls between the living room, bedroom two, and dining are shown as adobe. These adobe walls will increase the comfort level of the spaces.

Bedroom two could run into code problems in some towns. With the double glass doors opening into the sun porch the light should be ample. A skylight in the ceiling would improve the daylight factor.

This house is most efficient in the milder climates of southern New Mexico, Arizona, and southwest Texas. The large north portal in such areas will provide outdoor living space for six to seven months of the year.

DOS·RECÁMARA

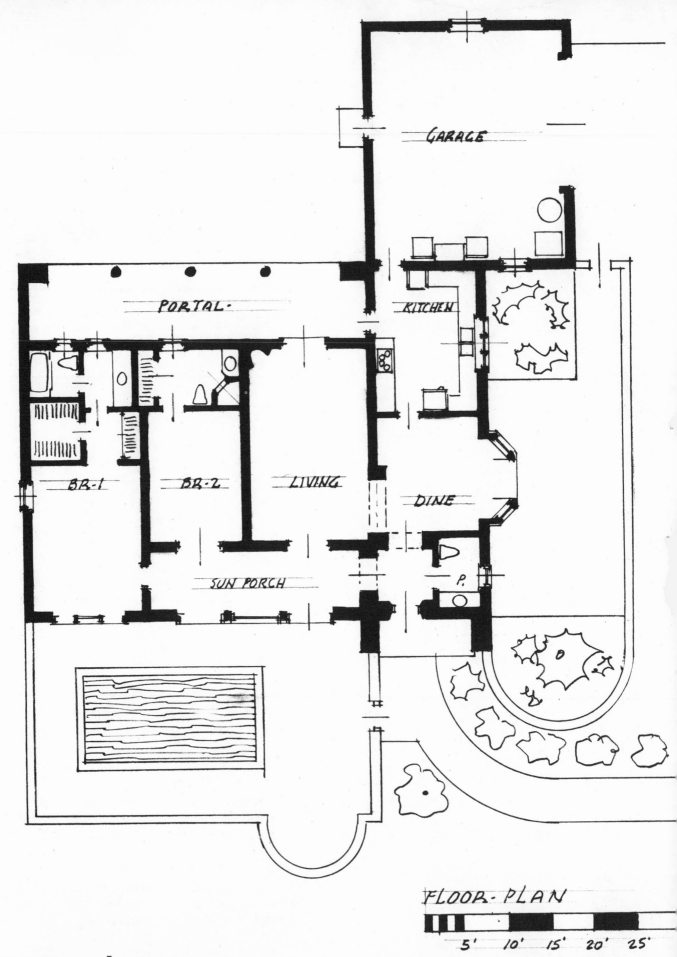

GARAGE

PORTAL·

KITCHEN

BR·1   BR·2   LIVING

DINE

SUN PORCH

P.

FLOOR·PLAN

5'   10'   15'   20'   25'

DOS·RECÁMARA·